JACK WARREN WADE, JR.

How to Reduce
Your Withholding
and
Increase Your
Take-Home Pay

COLLIER BOOKS
Macmillan Publishing Company
New York

TO my grandmothers,
Laura Patterson and
Bessie Obenshain,
For their Love and Devotion

Also by Jack Warren Wade, Jr.:
When You Owe the IRS

Macmillan Publishing Company
866 Third Avenue, New York, N.Y. 10022
Collier Macmillan Canada, Inc.

Library of Congress Cataloging in Publication Data
Wade, Jack Warren.
   How to reduce your withholding and increase your take-home pay.
   1. Withholding tax—Law and legislation—United States—Popular works.
2. Income tax—United States—Deductions.   3. Withholding tax—United States.   I. Title.
KF6436.Z9W32   1985   343.7305'242   84-23690
ISBN 0-02-008860-4   347.3035242

10 9 8 7 6 5 4 3 2 1

Printed in the United States of America

Special thanks to the following for their helpful suggestions to improve the manuscript:
Martha Gray, Lee Edmondson, Jim Lippold, and Stan Soltroff.

CONTENTS

| Form **W-4** (Rev. January 1985) | Department of the Treasury—Internal Revenue Service **Employee's Withholding Allowance Certificate** | OMB No. 1545-0010 Expires: 11-30-87 |

1 Type or print your full name

2 Your social security number

Home address (number and street or rural route)

City or town, State, and ZIP code

3 Marital Status
☐ Single ☐ Married
☐ Married, but withhold at higher Single rate
Note: If married, but legally separated, or spouse is a nonresident alien, check the Single box.

4 Total number of allowances you are claiming (from line F of the worksheet on page 2) . . . .

5 Additional amount, if any, you want deducted from each pay . . . . $

6 I claim exemption from withholding because (see instructions and check boxes below that apply):

a ☐ Last year I did not owe any Federal income tax and had a right to a full refund of **ALL** income tax withheld, **AND**

b ☐ This year I do not expect to owe any Federal income tax and expect to have a right to a full refund of **ALL** income tax withheld. If both a and b apply, enter the year effective and "EXEMPT" here ▶ | Year |

c If you entered "EXEMPT" on line 6b, are you a full-time student? . . . . ☐ Yes ☐ No

Under penalties of perjury, I certify that I am entitled to the number of withholding allowances claimed on this certificate, or if claiming exemption from withholding, that I am entitled to claim the exempt status.
Employee's signature ▶ .... Date ▶ ...., 19........

7 Employer's name and address **(Employer: Complete 7, 8, and 9 only if sending to IRS)**

8 Office code

9 Employer identification number

PREFACE

How to Use This Book

This is a self-instructional workbook designed to help you eliminate overpaying your federal income taxes, an event that occurs when you have more money withheld from your paycheck than is necessary to meet your tax liability. If your income tax refund check was over $200 last year, you were *overwithheld* on your withholding taxes, and you must read chapters 1, 2, and 3.

Overwithholding is a very common problem, as you will discover in Chapter 1. However, it is a problem than can be easily corrected by merely spending a few hours reading and working your way through this workbook. This book will not only teach you how the tax laws allow you to reduce your withholding and increase your take-home pay—but with the computational aids in each chapter, it will help you determine what the IRS requires as your legally permissible minimum amount of income tax withholding. Chapter 1 discusses all the reasons people typically give for being overwithheld, and the real reasons why they "loan" money to the government "interest-free" every year.

The key to almost all withholding problems centers around IRS Form W-4, "Employee's Withholding Allowance Certificate." In Chapter 2 you will not only learn how to compute all the withholding allowances you are legally entitled to claim, but you will make all your computations right in the text. The chapter follows the W-4 Worksheet line-by-line, in a format that is as easy to follow as counting from one to ten.

Chapter 3 is also must reading after you've computed your allowances in Chapter 2. Many taxpayers worry about being *under*withheld. There is sometimes the possibility of being *under*withheld when you claim all your legally permissible allowances. Chapter 3 will help you compute the maximum number of allowances that will *not* result in underwithholding. A worksheet has been specifically designed for this purpose and is included at the end of the chapter.

Chapters 4, 5, and 6 are special chapters for certain groups of taxpayers, and are not required reading for those without the applicable situations. Chapter 4 is only for those who have recently purchased a residence or made some type of increased mortgage commitment pertaining to their residence. Chapter 5 is only for those who work part of the year (not necessarily part-time), and Chapter 6 is for those who have dramatic or erratic shifts in their income. Skip those chapters if those situations don't apply to you.

At the end of each chapter in chapters 3 through 6 is a worksheet designed to help you eliminate some aspect of overwithholding. The worksheets are easy to follow and if you've read the examples in the chapters, you'll have no problem in using them. With the aid of a pocket calculator, you can make all your computations in the worksheets. The information from the worksheets can then be transferred either to the W-4 Worksheet (reverse side of the W-4) or the Form W-4 itself.

The only knowledges you will need are certain estimates of your deductions and tax credits for the current tax year, and of your income and your spouse's income, if married, and a basic understanding of the layout of a Form 1040, your individual tax return. A good place to start when making an estimate is with last years' tax return.

Besides your personal tax information, the book is self-contained with other applicable information such as the 1985 income tax withholding tables and the 1985 tax rate schedules. The appendixes have all of those tables, plus others that you may need, along with an explanation of how to use the Percentage Method Tables, an excercise only necessary for those using Chapter 6.

Unlike other books that purport to "save you money on your taxes" by either showing you deductions you don't qualify for, or discussing "schemes" that cost you more in the end than you'll ever save, this book covers a legal, legitimate, and simple technique that *over 70 million taxpayers can use.*

The overwithholding problem is, undoubtedly, the "sleeper problem" of the year. It has gotten virtually no press play, the IRS has ignored it, and it has gone unnoticed for years. It's ironic that 9 out of 10 wage-earning taxpayers spend great sums of money every year to wrangle their tax liability to its lowest level, yet will deliberately *overpay* hundreds, even thousands of dollars through their withholding.

If you overpay every year, you are always "loaning" money to the government, and this loan can exist up to 15 to 16 months, for an average of about $1,000 ($69 a month). Once you have increased your withholding allowances and eliminated your overwithholding, you will have recovered this $1,000 in the first 16 months. As long as you don't become overwithheld again, you will have recovered this money, and essentially "saved" this much on your taxes.

Good financial management dictates that you pay only your fair share or what is legally required. This book will help you to overcome the one big problem area that you can easily correct yourself without incurring additional risk or expense. For a few hours time, the simple techniques learned here may well prove to be a worthy return on your investment.

NOTE: In late 1984 the IRS released new personal exemption and zero bracket amounts to reflect a 4.1 percent indexing adjustment for inflation. Beginning in 1985 the personal exemption is increased to $1,040 from $1,000 and the zero bracket amounts are increased as follows:
- *Single, from $2,300 to $2,390*
- *Married filing jointly, from $3,400 to $3,540*
- *Married filing separately, from $1,700 to $1,770*
- *Head of household, from $2,300 to $2,390*
- *Qualifying widow(er), from $3,400 to $3,540.*

CHAPTER ONE

Why You Should Reduce Your Overwithholding

In 1984 the IRS paid out $58.8 billion in refund checks to 70.5 million taxpayers, for an average refund of $833. The United States is probably the only country in the world whose citizens not only pay their taxes voluntarily but some even deliberately *overpay* them, year after year after year.

THE NATURE OF THE PROBLEM

A lot of taxpayers are unaware that they can eliminate over-withholding. Many look on their overwithholding as the fault of the government, totally ignoring their own roles. In our tax system of voluntary compliance, individual taxpayers, and not the government, complete and file their own tax returns, reporting their share of the tax burden. They also tell their employers how much to withhold by filing a W-4 Certificate showing their marital status and how many allowances (or exemptions) they're entitled to claim.

Most taxpayers are unaware that they can eliminate their over-withholding by adjusting their W-4 Certificates to claim additional withholding allowances beyond those allowed for exemptions and dependents. For instance, are you aware that if you are single you can claim an *extra* withholding allowance (or exemption) just for being single? If you are married, are you aware that this special withholding allowance is also available when only one spouse is employed?

If you have a mortgage on a house, are you aware that you can reduce your withholding because of your mortgage interest and real-estate tax payments? If you are entitled to claim the child-care tax credit, are you aware that you can reduce your withholding now and increase your paycheck to help you meet those child-care expenses?

Obviously, few taxpayers understand this because the amount of taxes overwithheld has skyrocketed by almost 100 percent since 1977. The weak link appears to be the W-4 form, the "Employee's Withholding Allowance Certificate."

Most taxpayers are ignorant of the importance of the W-4 Certificate in tax planning for several reasons. First, about the only time they ever see a W-4 is when they are first hired. Few taxpayers will change their W-4s even when they know they can legally do so. Secondly, only a few taxpayers know how to fill out a W-4 Worksheet to compute additional withholding allowances. Almost any employer will admit that. And chances are that the employer knows little more than his employees. (When questioned, most employers will tell their new employees to put down "1" exemption!) Thirdly, the instructions on Form W-4 are written in a way that presumes the taxpayer knows as much about taxes as the IRS official who wrote them. (This has been a major complaint about many IRS publications, instructions, and forms.)

The ignorance about Form W-4 and related withholding terms can be illustrated easily. Just ask anyone how many *deductions* or how many *dependents* they're claiming, and you'll get an answer. But ask them how many *allowances* they're claiming and you'll get a puzzled look. You'll probably have to explain what you're talking about. (If you're still not sure what an allowance is, consider it to be an extra exemption worth $1,040. Chapter 2 has a complete discussion and definition of an allowance.)

The refund statistics prove that most employees have no idea how to use the W-4 to their best financial advantage. During the 1970s, a period of runaway, double-digit inflation and reduced earnings power, taxpaying wage earners were being pushed into increasingly higher tax brackets. This caused a proportional increase in overwithholding as they had a higher percentage of income tax withheld. The General Accounting Office has reported that 80 to 90 percent of all taxpayers subject to withholding were overwithheld throughout the 1970s. But these statistics never decreased. To fully appreciate how far out of hand the problem has become, look at the statistics in the following chart.

Fiscal Year	No. of Individual Income Taxpayers (*millions*)	Total Amount of Refunds (*billions*)	Average Refund
1978	65.7	$32.95	$495
1979	65.6	34.9	518
1980	72.3	44.4	614
1981	71.3	48.4	679
1982	71.6	55.1	769
1983	73.7	61.2	830
1984(incomplete)	70.5	58.8	833

Over seven of every ten taxpayers get a refund check, and almost nine out of every ten employees are overwithheld! How many of those refunds come from employees who actually *prefer* to be overwithheld? And how many of those refunds come from employees who would rather have that money paid to them during the year when they could most use it? How many employees are deliberately overwithheld because they are afraid of owing the IRS?

The IRS does not now have an accurate answer to those questions, but by discussing your responsibilities, rights, and options with regard to the withholding process, we can give you an opportunity to answer them for yourself.

WHY TAXPAYERS OVERWITHHOLD

One theory of the root cause of overwithholding blames a prevalent *fear of the IRS*: fear of being audited; fear of not being able to pay when taxes are due; fear of going to jail; or fear of the awesome enforcement power of the IRS. But such fears are more covert and subconscious because rarely does anyone admit that "fear of the IRS" is their primary motivation for overwithholding. On the overt, conscious level, other reasons are usually advanced to justify or rationalize the practice.

It would appear, though, that overwithholding continues to exist, and even increase each year, more out of a conscious lack of action to correct it than a conscious effort to cause it. This occurs because of an overall lack of knowledge concerning withholding allowances and their effect on the withholding process.

Let's look at some of the justifications used by taxpayers to explain why they continue to overwithhold year after year. These are typical responses to the question, "Why are you overwithheld on your taxes?"

Response: "I don't want to be audited!"

Analysis: This is a false argument. There is no proof to substantiate the belief that taxpayers who are overwithheld are less likely to be audited. A counterargument could be made that taxpayers with large refunds are more likely to be audited because the IRS suspects the larger the refund, the bigger the cheating. But neither of these arguments has any merit whatsoever. Tax returns are generally selected for audit under IRS's computer selection program called Discriminant Function, a highly sophisticated and secret program that measures probabilities with key relationships of items on the return that are based on historical precedent. It is too scientific and sophisticated to be based on something as irrelevant as the size of a refund check.

Response: "I don't want to owe the IRS."

Analysis: Who says you have to owe the IRS? It's not a question of the IRS owing you $833 or *you* owing the IRS $833. By claiming the proper number of withholding allowances, and using the adjustment worksheet in Chapter 3, you can compute your withholding allowances to being very close to par with your expected tax liability. And what if you do miscalculate? It's no crime to owe the IRS *any* amount of money. They will not lock you up, you will not have to go to court, and they will not even penalize you if your withholding is within 20 percent of your final tax liability computed on your 1040. Also, they give you time and opportunity to pay before they get too nasty. (Besides, if you get into any real trouble, just get a copy of my book, *When You Owe The IRS*.)

Response: "I like getting a large refund check."

Analysis: The persons who give this response are probably so unaware of their tax situation that they probably not only don't know how many allowances they are currently claiming, but it's a safe bet that they don't even know what an allowance is.

You should realize that your refund check is neither a bonus nor a windfall gift from the IRS. (This attitude is prevalent now.) Many taxpayers pride themselves on how large their refunds are, as if they were implying that the IRS was being especially good to them and not so good to someone who didn't get as large a refund. Some taxpayers are so devious in boasting of their large refunds that they seem to be trying to impress their friends with their profound knowledge of tax law. Isn't it interesting that while it is not socially acceptable for you to brag about your income, it is socially acceptable for you to brag about the size of your refund check.

Response: "I use my refund check as a forced savings."

Analysis: This is probably the most prevalent response given. It's rooted in the naiveté of those who think that there are no other opportunities for saving money or believe that they don't possess the discipline to save voluntarily. This response is usually followed up with testimony about how their "forced savings," in the form of a green Treasury check, was used to finance their vacation or as a down payment on a new car, new furniture, or a new house. Notice that these people are still on "cloud nine" when they try to convince you that they never could have done it without the IRS. Unfortunately, these people know little about money management: They probably spend their entire check as soon as they get it.

A much better technique for saving money is to have your employer send an allotment to your credit union or savings account. For those who think it is their patriotic duty to "lend" their savings to the government, they should consider using the extra $69 a month (or $833 a year) to purchase U.S. Savings Bonds. They are easy to purchase and a bit inconvenient to cash, but at least you get interest payments on your "forced savings." If you're afraid you'll run right out and cash them as soon as you get them, give them to a third party for safekeeping with instructions to let you have possession only at a certain date.

An alternative to overwithholding gives you several advantages: First, you are paid interest on your money; second, the money's available for emergencies or for whenever you need it. When you're overwithheld, you can't retrieve a penny of it until you file your tax return the following year.

WHAT INFLUENCES THE SIZE OF YOUR REFUND CHECK

The amount of your refund check is simply the result of three variables:

- the amount of your taxable income;
- the total of your allowable deductions, exemptions, and credits; and
- the amount of income tax you have withheld.

Any combination of those variables will change your refund to make it either higher or lower.

The amount of your taxable income is probably a given. Anyone paid a standard salary or wage knows how much money he makes or will make, and, except for salespeople on commissions, few tax-payers have the opportunity to increase their income at will. The amount of deductions, exemptions, and credits claimed on your tax return may also be a given, or it may be the result of a conflict between you and your conscience. (One universally accepted theory is that everyone cheats on their taxes a little.)

As April 15 approaches every year, taxpayers spend a tremendous amount of time, energy, and expense attempting to reduce their tax liability and thereby increase their refund checks. (Is there a feeling that the large refund check is compensation for the April 14 "midnight oil ritual"?)

But almost forgotten in the rush is the last variable in the amount of refund you get: the amount of income tax you have withheld. Obviously, two different taxpayers with the exact same tax liability may get different refund checks, depending on how much income tax was withheld. The taxpayer with the most income tax withheld will receive the larger refund, and the taxpayer with the lesser amount of tax withheld will receive the smaller refund.

So when you hear that your next-door neighbor, who makes as much money as you do and who has about the same standard of living that you have, gets a larger refund check, don't worry that he might have known about some deductions that you didn't know about. He probably just had more income tax withheld than you did.

The amount of income tax you direct to be withheld should solely be a function of your *expected tax liability*, and not of your inability to understand the W-4 form or of your lack of discipline to save for a rainy day.

Consider, for instance, that over twelve million taxpayers are self-employed and do *not* have income tax withheld from their paychecks. Instead, they must estimate and pay what they owe four times a year. (The IRS collects over $83 billion a year this way.) This means that they must not only have the discipline to save enough money to pay their income taxes four times a year, but they must also save enough to pay their Social Security taxes at the same time.

Those who have taxes withheld from their paychecks could learn a valuable point from self-employed individuals who do not have withholding. Self-employed taxpayers are probably more attuned to money management than employed taxpayers because their income tends to fluctuate more with the various changes in the economy. Less than 50 percent of self-employed taxpayers overpay their taxes. They would rather underpay the IRS slightly and risk the imposition of a civil penalty for doing so. They know that they can usually make better use of their money during the course of the year, even if it's only to put it into a savings account.

Important: *If you are overwithheld every year, you should increase your withholding allowances to cut back on your tax withholding and increase your net income.*

THE GOVERNMENT'S ROLE IN OVERWITHHOLDING

The IRS is clearly aware that there are substantial increases every year in the number of refund checks issued, the amount of taxes refunded, and the size of the average refund check. (The chart on page 11 clearly dramatizes this.) Officially, the IRS acknowledges that overwithholding is a burden to the government. It forces the Treasury Department to borrow substantial sums of money from the marketplace during a short period of time (mostly during March, April, and May) in order to pay those enormous refunds. There is no question that this extra borrowing disrupts the financial markets because government borrowing competes with corporate borrowing for a fixed amount of investment money. Because the U.S. government has the power to borrow as much money as it needs, it can also pay interest rates as high as it wants or as high as the market demands. Within the past few years we have seen U.S. Treasury Bills pay short-term interest rates as high as 17 percent, while corporate bonding issues at lower rates went unsold. The

U.S. government may be able to extend its outstanding debt ceiling to an almost incomprehensible $1.5 trillion, but corporations are restricted in the amount of money they can borrow.

But some taxpayers speculate that the government isn't really interested in having too many taxpayers cut back on their over-withholding. After all, the extra $58.8 billion in overwithholding is essentially an "interest-free loan" to the government. In fact, over-withholding *is a loan* and *has* to be viewed as a loan, because the following year it *has* to be repaid in the form of refund checks. So the process continues, year after year.

You don't have to be a financial genius to see that it is to the government's advantage that overwithholding continues to some extent. A major, sudden cessation of overwithholding would force the government to step up its borrowing to compensate for the sudden loss of income. But the eventual long-term impact of a cessation of overwithholding may be beneficial for the financial markets, since it would reduce the enormous borrowing that occurs during the tax-filing season and spread it out more evenly through-out the year. Under the present situation, the government is get-ting an interest-free ride in the amount of $58.8 billion each year.

The IRS has made efforts to alert taxpayers to the overwithhold-ing problem. Several times a year they issue press releases and send flyers with refund checks asking taxpayers to reevaluate their with-holding status. They also send notices to employers asking them to inform their employees of their right to adjust their withholding if too much tax is being withheld. But one look at the statistics shows that the effort is a failure, and in the absence of major public awareness of the situation, overwithholding will probably continue to rise.

If the IRS were really serious about stopping the tremendous amount of overwithholding, they would initiate an educational campaign to teach people how to complete a W-4 Worksheet and compute their additional withholding allowances. Such a campaign would go far to dispel the notion that they are more interested in maintaining their "fear" image than they are in solving this problem.

YOUR ROLE

Everyone is concerned about taxes, but for many taxpayers there are only so many things they can legally do to minimize their tax bite. Tax shelters are only for those in the 50 percent tax bracket, and deductions only return a small percentage of every dollar spent. So *the only option available to many taxpayers is to reduce their withholding legally to increase their net income.* In effect, over 70.5 million taxpayers can give themselves an average pay raise of $833 a year (or $69 a month) by simply adjusting their withholding. This could be the simplest and easiest available method to obtain a raise in pay.

It should be pointed out that even though you may be over-withheld an average $69 a month, or $833 over twelve months, your overwithholding doesn't stop there. While you are over-withholding from January through December of any particular year, you will most likely not receive your refund check until March or April of the following year. This means that if you are over-withheld the subsequent year also, your overwithholding could exceed, on the average, $1,000 if you count the additional withholding for the months of January, February, March, and April of the subsequent year.

Think about what you could do with $1,000 over the next sixteen months. Sixty-nine dollars a month would go a long way to reduce charge account bills or helping to pay rising gasoline or utility costs.

Remember that while you may be lending the government $69 a month interest free, you are paying 18 percent or more a year to your credit card companies. A more practical approach for your family budget would be to determine if it would be more economical for you to have the $69 a month now or some time next year. You must evaluate your own needs and finances. Remember, though, the government doesn't *make* you overwithhold, and you have the right to discontinue the practice. Ask yourself why you should overpay the IRS when you don't do it with your other creditors. Obviously, you want to pay what you owe, but why pay what you don't owe?

INTEREST ON REFUNDS

Many taxpayers resent being overwithheld because the IRS doesn't give them interest on their refunds. The IRS does not pay interest on refunds for a simple and obvious reason: *You are responsible for your own overwithholding.* Unless the IRS makes a mistake on the tax tables (and this has happened), or unless your employer makes a bookkeeping error, the responsibility is totally yours and totally within your control to correct. All it takes is a little time and effort to sit down at the beginning of each year and figure out how much you're going to earn, how much income tax is going to be withheld, and approximately what your income tax liability will be. If you received tax refunds in previous years and estimate that you'll get one for the current tax year, you are not claiming enough with-holding allowances, causing your employer to withhold too much income tax. If your last refund check was more than $200, *you are unquestionably loaning too much money to the government.*

The IRS does pay interest on a refund when it has not been able to process the tax return and issue the refund check within forty-five days after the due date of the return, or within forty-five days after the return was actually filed if filed after the due date. For late returns, interest is computed back to the date of actual filing of the return, not the due date. But the obvious and important point is that while you may have to pay interest on any money you owe the IRS, the IRS does not have to pay you interest just because you paid-in too much tax.

CHAPTER TWO

Computing Your Maximum Permissible Withholding Allowances

If you don't understand the terminology on your W-4 form, don't worry—most taxpayers are just as confused as you are. Hardly anyone knows the difference between a dependent, a deduction, an exemption, and an allowance. But before we proceed with adjusting your withholding, it is important that you understand what these words mean.

THE TERMINOLOGY OF WITHHOLDING

An exemption is a specified amount of money that will not be taxed. For instance, the tax code grants exemptions of $1,040 (formerly $1,000) for yourself and for your spouse, and additional $1,040 exemptions for other situations such as being blind, and for being over age 65. This means that no tax is paid on each $1,040 exemption claimed. On Form 1040 you subtract the total amount of exemptions from your adjusted gross income before computing your tax.

An exemption of $1,040 is also allowed for each dependent that meets five dependency tests set by the IRS. You are not allowed to claim the extra $1,040 exemption for dependents who are over age 65 and/or blind. *The dependent used for the $1,040 income tax exemption on Form 1040 is the same dependent used on Form W-4* when computing withholding allowances. In order to qualify as a *dependent*, these five tests must be met:

- You must provide more than half of the dependent's total support during the calendar year.
- The dependent must not have gross income in excess of $1,000 for the year. This test does not apply to a child who was under 19 at the end of the year or to a child who is a student, regardless of age. But be careful: A dependent who earns more than $1,000 in a year may have provided more than half of his own support.
- The dependent must either be a relative as specified by the tax code or must live in your household for the entire year.
- The dependent must be a U.S. citizen, resident, or national or be a resident of Canada or Mexico for some part of the calendar year.
- A married dependent cannot file a joint return with his or her spouse.

A dependent must meet each of those five tests before you are entitled to the $1,040 exemption.

A deduction is an expense item that is subtracted from your adjusted gross income when computing your taxable income, the amount on which your tax liability is computed. Commonly known deductions include medical expenses, taxes, interest expenses, charitable contributions, and casualty or theft losses. (Just to make things more confusing, in tax language the items that are deducted on your tax return preceding the adjusted gross income line are really "adjustments" rather than deductions.)

Almost everyone is familiar with the old *standard deduction* that you could subtract from your income when your itemized deductions were not large enough. The IRS did away with this standard deduction and replaced it with the *zero bracket amount*, a part of your income also not subject to taxation. The IRS incorporated the old standard deduction dollar amounts into the tax tables so that only the total of your itemized deductions exceeding the new zero bracket amount are deductible. For example, a married couple filing a joint return who have $6,000 in itemized deductions can deduct $2,460 from their adjusted gross income—the amount of their itemized deductions that exceeds their zero bracket amount of $3,540 ($6,000 − $3,540 = $2,460). This is important to know because *extra withholding allowances are allowed for itemized deductions that exceed your zero bracket amount plus $520.* (The IRS threw in the $520 to compensate for their rounding instructions on the form W-4 Worksheet. You'll learn more about this later.)

An allowance is a relative term, used only on Form W-4, that is related to the amount of income tax that will be deducted from your paycheck. It has absolutely no meaning for purposes of completing your tax return. One allowance is given for each $1,040 of income not subject to being taxed. Your number of withholding allowances is computed on the W-4 Worksheet. The greater the number of allowances you have, the less income tax will be withheld. Consider a withholding allowance an additional reduction in withholding, as allowances are given the same weight as exemptions.

The IRS allows withholding allowances for exemptions, dependents, excess itemized deductions, alimony, and for tax credits or adjustments. As you can see, a dependent can be an exemption and a dependent can be an allowance, but an allowance is not limited to dependents or exemptions. If, for example, you claim the number of withholding allowances equal only to the number of your dependents or exemptions, that may be why you are having too much tax withheld.

CATEGORIES OF ALLOWANCES

There are five categories under which withholding allowances may be claimed on Form W-4:

- *Personal Allowances.* Just as you can claim an exemption on Form 1040 for yourself, for being blind, and for being over age 65, so may you claim an allowance for each of these on Form W-4. You can claim these same exemptions for your spouse on W-4, but only if your spouse does not work or does not claim them on his or her W-4.

  Single taxpayers who hold more than one job may not claim

the same allowances on each job. Married taxpayers can only claim the personal exemption of their spouses as long as their spouses aren't claiming it with their employer.

- *Special Withholding Allowance.* This is one of the biggest surprises to most people. The special withholding allowance is an extra allowance available to single taxpayers who have only one job, and to married taxpayers who have only one job and whose spouses do not work. The special withholding allowance is only for withholding purposes and has no counterpart on Forms 1040, 1040 EZ, or 1040A. For those who qualify for the special withholding allowance, it *must be claimed* to prevent over-withholding. If you don't claim it, you will probably be over-withheld several hundred dollars over a twelve-month period. Many cases of overwithholding are due to being uninformed about the special withholding allowance.

- *Allowances for Dependents.* You may claim a withholding allowance for each dependent that you can claim on your income tax return. (Remember the five dependency tests? They apply here also.)

- *Allowances for Certain Tax Credits.* A tax credit is a dollar-for-dollar offset against your tax liability. In effect, the government is reimbursing you 100 percent of the amount you spent on an allowable credit. Tax credits not only lower your tax liability but also increase your tax refund by a comparable amount. To avoid having too much income tax withheld, you can claim extra allowances for the value of those credits. The number of allowances you can claim is based on an estimate of the amount of money you will earn during the year in conjunction with an estimate of the amount of tax credits that you will be able to deduct at the end of the year. The reverse side of the W-4 form contains a tax credit table to compute the number of allowances you will be able to claim. The tax credits that you especially need to know about are the earned income credit, the credit for child- and dependent-care expenses, the credit for the elderly, and the credit allowed for residential energy items.

• *Allowances for Estimated Itemized Deductions and Adjustments to Income.* You are allowed to claim additional withholding allowances if you have an amount of itemized deductions that exceeds your zero bracket amount, and for adjustments to income, such as alimony, moving expenses, IRA contributions, or employee business expenses. (Alimony payments are deductible by the spouse making the payments and are taxable to the spouse receiving the payment.) The reverse side of Form W-4 also includes a worksheet for determining the total number of additional withholding allowances you can claim.

Important: *Your goal should be to claim all the withholding allowances on Form W-4 to which you are legally entitled without having too much or too little tax withheld by the end of each tax year.*

ESTIMATING YOUR ALLOWANCES

Now that you have an understanding of what allowances are, we are going to help you compute all the allowances you are legally entitled to claim. In Chapter 3 you will learn how to adjust those allowances so that you don't become underwithheld.

If you've looked at the W-4 form, you've probably noticed that the instructions are in small print and the tables and worksheets look rather complex and difficult to use. And if you've avoided using the W-4 Worksheet because you thought you needed a tax lawyer to decipher it for you, you should congratulate yourself for buying this book. You will find that by following an orderly progression of steps, as outlined here, the process will be easy and the effort well worth it.

As you proceed through this chapter you will be making computations right in this book. On page 30 is reprinted the "Worksheet to Figure Your Withholding Allowances to be Entered on Line 4 of Form W-4." This worksheet, taken from the back of Form

W-4, will be your final worksheet for computing your allowances.

You will be referred back to this page numerous times as the number of allowances you compute for lines A, B, C, D, E, and F will be transferred to this W-4 Worksheet. When the total on Line F has been determined, you will have computed all the withholding allowances you are legally entitled to claim. That figure should be carried to Line 4 of your W-4 Certificate.

When you've computed the necessary information for your W-4, you should sign it and submit it to your employer, and you probably will have increased your allowances and reduced your withholding.

SOME WITHHOLDING BASICS

On or before your first day on the job, your employer is required to ask you to submit a signed W-4 Certificate specifying your marital status and the number of withholding allowances you are claiming. Your W-4 is effective your first paycheck and remains in effect until you file a new one or leave that job.

If you fail to file a Form W-4, your employer must withhold taxes from your earnings at the "single" rate, even if the employer knows you're entitled to more withholding allowances.

With your W-4 in hand, your employer uses an IRS chart or table for computing your withholding. There are several tables and charts for the different methods he may use and you will learn more about these methods in Appendix 1. The actual amount withheld is figured on your gross wages before any deductions are taken for Social Security, union dues, insurances, etc. This amount is determined by the number of your withholding allowances claimed on your W-4 with consideration for your marital status and the amount you earned.

The IRS says that the withholding rates are designed to have the right amount of tax withheld from your pay, if you:

- work all year and earn about the same amount each pay period.
- have income mainly from one job (or one job at a time) to report on your tax return.
- do not have a large amount of income from any other source, and
- claim the correct number of allowances on Form W-4.

YOUR RESPONSIBILITIES

Events are always occurring that will change the exemptions, deductions, and credits that you can take on your tax return. IRS regulations require that you stay attuned to your number of withholding allowances and make adjustments accordingly.

For instance, if on any day during the calendar year you find that the number of allowances you are entitled to claim is *less* than you are presently claiming, you *must* submit a new W-4 within ten days, reducing your allowances accordingly. Some of the situations that may occur are:

- You have been using the personal exemption allowances for your spouse, but either you are no longer considered married for tax purposes or your spouse is now claiming his/her own personal exemptions.
- You have been claiming an allowance for a dependent but no longer expect to provide more than half the dependent's support.
- You have been claiming an allowance for your child, but he or she will be 19 years old by the end of the year, is not a student, and will earn more than $1,000 during the year.
- You have been claiming allowances for your estimated deductions and credits, but you discover that they will be less than expected.

If, on any day during the calendar year, you discover that you are *entitled to claim more withholding allowances* than what you are claiming, you *may* submit a new W-4 to your employer. Your employer can put it into effect as soon as it is practical for him to do so, but the IRS allows him the discretion to wait longer.

The IRS has *status determination days* that occur on January 1, May 1, July 1, and October 1. If you turn in your new W-4 at least thirty days before the status determination days, your employer must honor your W-4 on the first payday on or after that status determination day. If you do not turn it in thirty days before, your employer can wait until the first payday after the next status determination date.

A typical event that may cause an increase in withholding allowances is a birth or a marriage. IRS regulations, however, prohibit you from increasing your allowances *in anticipation of* either event. You must wait until the day the event occurs before you can adjust your W-4.

Another typical event that may entitle you to claim more allowances is the purchase of a house or a condominium, either for the first time or for a "trade up." In most instances under these situations, you will probably be taking on the added liability of increased mortgage and real estate tax payments. Increased mortgage interest and real estate tax payments most assuredly warrant an increase in withholding allowances. For some, it's a matter of economics: They need the benefit of the tax reduction caused by the increased deductions to help make the payments.

(If you bought this book because you have purchased a house for the first time, or you have "traded up" and need help with your W-4, you must read Chapter four. The IRS has new rules that will help you even more specifically than the information in this chapter. But don't bypass this chapter. You need to first learn how to complete the W-4 Worksheet.)

UNDERWITHHOLDING CAUTIONS

If at some time this year you become aware of events that will cause you to be eligible for *fewer* allowances *next year*, you *must* file a new

W-4 by December 1 of this year. If the change occurs in December, you have ten days to file a new W-4. Some of the situations that may occur are listed below:

- You have been claiming extra allowances due to child-care expenses, moving expenses, or large medical bills, and you know you will *not* have these expenses next year.
- You were claiming an extra allowance because of savings from income averaging, but your income has stabilized and you will not qualify for income averaging next year.
- You were claiming the personal exemption allowances for your spouse or the dependent's allowances for your children last year, and a death of one of them has resulted in a loss of that allowance this year.

Some taxpayers run the risk of having too little tax withheld when they hold more than one job at a time or when they and their spouses are both employed. It also happens frequently when they have other taxable income that is not subject to withholding, such as alimony, interest, dividends, capital gains, rents, or royalties.

The IRS says that there are three things you can do if you are underwithheld:

- You could claim fewer allowances, even down to zero.
- You could have additional amounts withheld.
- You could check the box on your W-4 marked "Married, but withhold at higher single rate," if you are currently having tax withheld at the "married" rate.

Underwithholding, however, is not the subject of this book,* since *overwithholding is the major problem* for 71 million taxpayers.

---

*If you are underwithheld, you may want to read my book *When You Owe the IRS*, to handle IRS collection procedures.

CALCULATING EVERY PERMISSIBLE ALLOWANCE

The IRS says, "If you usually have a large refund when you file your tax return, you may be having too much tax withheld. You can usually correct this by filing a new Form W-4 claiming more of the allowances you are permitted to claim." The rest of this chapter is devoted to doing this, by focusing on the reverse side of Form W-4, the part entitled "Worksheet to Figure Your Withholding Allowances to be Entered on Line 4 of Form W-4" (see the following page).

This worksheet is a computational aid designed to help you determine all the withholding allowances the IRS will allow you to claim. It looks complicated, and probably is to most people, but if it is dissected part by part and line by line, a "method to the madness" will be discovered and the form will not be the ordeal that it appears to be.

This chapter utilizes a self-instructional approach that allows you to focus your time and energy on those portions that apply to you. On the following pages are line-by-line instructions and computations. Follow the instructions carefully, and write your responses in the places specifically provided for them. The sections that apply to your situation should be so marked in the boxes indicated in the related instructions. For sections that don't apply to you, you should mark the box with an "X." This will help if you're interrupted and need to find your place again, or when referring back to sections you've already covered.

IRS Cautions

Before tackling the line-by-line allowances on the worksheet, the IRS wants you to heed the following cautions:

- If you are single and hold more than one job, you may not claim the same allowances with more than one employer at the same time. But you can split up the total number of allowances you're legally entitled to claim.
- If you are married, and both you and your spouse are em-

Line 5 of Form W-4

Additional amount, if any, you want deducted from each pay. — If you are not having enough tax withheld from your pay, you may ask your employer to withhold more by filling in an additional amount on line 5. Often, married couples, both of whom are working, and persons with two or more jobs need to have additional tax withheld. You may also need to have additional tax withheld because you have income other than wages, such as interest and dividends, capital gains, rents, alimony received, taxable social security benefits, etc. Estimate the amount you will be underwithheld and divide that amount by the number of pay periods in the year. Enter the additional amount you want withheld each pay period on line 5.

Line 6 of Form W-4

Exemption from withholding. — You can claim exemption from withholding only if last year you did not owe any Federal income tax and had a right to a refund of all income tax withheld, **and** this year you do not expect to owe any Federal income tax and expect to have a right to a refund of all income tax withheld. If you qualify, check Boxes 6a and b, write the year exempt status is effective and "EXEMPT" on line 6b, and answer Yes or No to the question on line 6c

If you want to claim exemption from withholding next year, you must file a new W-4 with your employer on or before February 15 of next year. If you are not having Federal income tax withheld this year, but expect to have a tax liability next year, the law requires you to give your employer a new W-4 by December 1 of this year. If you are covered by social security, your employer must withhold social security tax.

Your employer must send to IRS any W-4 claiming more than 14 withholding allowances or claiming exemption from withholding if the wages are expected to usually exceed $200 a week. The employer is to complete Boxes 7, 8, and 9 only on copies of the W-4 sent to IRS.

Table 1—For Figuring Your Withholding Allowances For Estimated Tax Credits and Income Averaging (Line E)

Estimated Salaries and Wages from All sources	Single Employees		Head of Household Employees		Married Employees (When Spouse not Employed)		Married Employees (When Both Spouses are Employed)	
	(A)	(B)	(A)	(B)	(A)	(B)	(A)	(B)
Under $15,000	$ 90	$150	$ 30	$150	$ 50	$120	$ 0	$120
15,000-25,000	120	250	0	250	70	170	310	170
25,001-35,000	190	300	0	300	130	250	800	220
35,001-45,000	250	370	0	370	170	320	1,500	250
45,001-55,000	690	370	0	370	230	340	2,210	330
55,001-65,000	1,470	370	220	370	310	370	3,020	330
Over 65,000	2,460	370	920	370	680	370	3,400	370

Worksheet to Figure Your Withholding Allowances to be Entered on Line 4 of Form W-4

A Personal allowances   . . . . ▶ **A**

B Special withholding allowance (not to exceed 1 allowance—see instructions on page 1) . . . . . ▶ **B**

C Allowances for dependents   . . . . ▶ **C**

If you are not claiming any deductions or credits, skip lines D and E.

D Allowances for estimated deductions:

1 Enter the total amount of your estimated itemized deductions, alimony payments, qualified retirement contributions including IRA and Keogh (H.R. 10) plans, deduction for a married couple when both work, business losses including net operating loss carryovers, moving expenses, employee business expenses, penalty on early withdrawal of savings, and charitable contributions for nonitemizers for the year . . . . ▶ **1** $

2 If you do not plan to itemize deductions, enter $500 on line D2. If you plan to itemize, find your total estimated salaries and wages amount in the left column of the table below. (Include salaries and wages of both spouses.) Read across to the right and find the amount from the column that applies to you. Enter that amount on line D2. . . . . ▶ **2** $

Estimated salaries and wages from all sources:	Single and Head of Household Employees (only one job)	Married Employees (one spouse working and one job only)	Employees with more than one job or Married Employees with both spouses working [1]
Under $15,000	. $2,800	. $3,900	40%
15,000-35,000	. 2,800	. 3,900	23%
35,001-50,000	. 8% } of estimated salaries and wages	. 3,900	20% } of estimated salaries and wages
Over $50,000	. 10% }	. 7% of estimated salaries and wages	18%

3 Subtract line D2 from line D1 (But not less than zero) . . . . ▶ **3** $

4 Divide the amount on line D3 by $1,000 (increase any fraction to the next whole number). Enter here . . . ▶ **D**

E Allowances for tax credits and income averaging: use Table 1 above for figuring withholding allowances

1 Enter tax credits, excess social security tax withheld, and tax reduction from income averaging $

2 Enter the column (A) amount from Table 1 for your salary range and filing status (single, etc.). However, enter 0 if you claim 1 or more allowances on line D4 . . . . $

3 Subtract line 2 from line 1 (If zero or less, do not complete lines 4 and 5) . . . . . . $

4 Find the column (B) amount from Table 1 for your salary range and filing status . . . . $

5 Divide line 3 by line 4. Increase any fraction to the next whole number. This is the maximum number of withholding allowances for tax credits and income averaging. Enter here . . . . ▶ **E**

Example: A taxpayer who expects to file a Federal income tax return as a single person estimates annual wages of $12,000 and tax credits of $650. The $12,000 falls in the wage bracket of under $15,000. The value in column (A) was 90. Subtracting this from the estimated credits of 650 leaves 560. The value in column (B) is 150. Dividing 560 by 150 gives 3.7. Since any fraction is increased to the next whole number, show 4 on line E.

F Total (add lines A through E). Enter total here and on line 4 of Form W-4 . . . . ▶ **F**

[1] If you earn 10% or less of your total wages from other jobs or one spouse earns 10% or less of the couple's combined total wages, you can use the "Single and Head of Household Employees (only one job)" or "Married Employees (one spouse working and one job only)" table, whichever is appropriate

ployed, you may *not* both claim the same allowances with your respective employers at the same time. A husband and wife who file a joint return this year may total up their allowances and allocate them any way they decide, including all to one spouse and none to the other spouse. This can be decided after reaching a total on Line F on the form W-4 Worksheet. Use the following worksheet to determine the total number of allowances due you as a couple.

• If you are married and filed separate returns last year *and* expect to file separate returns this year, you must compute your allowances separately based on your own individual wages and allowable items.

LINE A. PERSONAL ALLOWANCES

Worksheet to Figure Your Withholding Allowances To Be Entered on Line 4 of Form W-4	
A Personal allowances . . . . ▶	A
B Special withholding allowance (not to exceed 1 allowance—see instructions on page 1) . . . . ▶	B
C Allowances for dependents . . . . ▶	C

On line A you are going to compute your personal withholding allowances. Put check marks in the following boxes that apply to you:

☐ For yourself. Everyone should check here.

☐ If you will be 65 or older on the last day of the year.

☐ If you are blind, i.e., either you cannot see better than $^{20}/_{200}$ in your better eye with glasses, or your field of vision is not more than 20 degrees.

If you are married *and* either:

• your spouse is *not* employed; or
• your spouse is employed, but *you* are going to claim the allowances and not him/her; or
• your spouse is employed, but you are computing all your allowances together, and later will decide how to split them up:

Check the following boxes that apply to you:

☐ For your spouse.

☐ If your spouse will be 65 or older on the last day of the year.

☐ If your spouse is blind because of the same criteria as above.

Total number of boxes checked above: _____

☐ Enter the *total* number of boxes checked above on Line A of the W-4 Worksheet on page 30. The maximum allowable allowances on Line A is six. Check this box when you have made that entry.

LINE B. SPECIAL WITHHOLDING ALLOWANCE

Worksheet to Figure Your Withholding Allowances to be Entered on Line 4 of Form W-4

A Personal allowances	▶	A
B Special withholding allowance (not to exceed 1 allowance—see instructions on page 1)	▶	B
C Allowances for dependents	▶	C

If you are not claiming any deductions or credits, skip lines D and E.

You may be entitled to claim *one* special withholding allowance. Read the following and put a check mark in the box that applies to your situation:

☐ If you are single (or married but considered single for tax purposes—check with the IRS for clarification) and have only one job.

☐ If you are married, have only one job, and your spouse is *not* employed.

☐ If you are married and you or your spouse (or both) have another part-time job(s), but the earnings from the other job(s) are 10 percent or less of the total combined earnings of you and your spouse from all jobs.

   Example: On your full-time job you earn $26,000 a year, and on your part-time job you earn $2,800 a year. You can still claim the special withholding allowance because $2,800 is 10 percent or less of the *combined* earnings of $28,800.

Example: On your full-time job you earn $32,000, and on your part-time job you earn $1,500. Your spouse also works part-time and earns $2,000. You can still claim the special withholding allowance because the $3,500 earned from *both* part-time jobs is 10 percent or less of the *combined* earnings of $35,500.

☐ Enter a "1" on Line B of your W-4 Worksheet on page 30 if you checked any of the three boxes for the situations above. (Put a check mark in the box at left when you have done this.) You can never have more than "one" special withholding allowance. (Remember, this is for withholding purposes only. You cannot claim the special withholding allowance on your tax return.)

LINE C. ALLOWANCES FOR DEPENDENTS

Skip this section if you have no dependents. Go directly to the instructions for Line D.

A   Personal allowances . . . . ▶ A
B   Special withholding allowance (not to exceed 1 allowance—see instructions on page 1) . . . . ▶ B
C   Allowances for dependents . . . . ▶ C
    If you are not claiming any deductions or credits, skip lines D and E.
D   Allowances for estimated deductions:

On page 21 we briefly outlined the five support tests necessary to claim a dependent. If you have any further questions about whether someone qualifies as your dependent, you should either contact your local IRS office for information or refer to IRS Publication #17, "Your Federal Income Tax," Chapter 3, or IRS Publication #501, "Exemptions."

List below the names, ages, relationship, and whether the five support tests have been meet for each dependent. Put a check mark in the corresponding box.

**Meets Five
Dependency Tests?   Name of Dependent   Age   Relationship**
(✔ = yes)

☐   _____   ____   _____

☐   _____   ____   _____

☐   _____   ____   _____

☐   _____   ____   _____

☐   _____   ____   _____

☐   _____   ____   _____

☐   _____   ____   _____

TOTAL number of boxes checked above: _____

☐ Enter total number of boxes checked above on Line C of the
W-4 Worksheet on page 30, then check the box.

LINE D. ALLOWANCES FOR ESTIMATED DEDUCTIONS

A   Personal allowances . . . . ▶ | A |
B   Special withholding allowance (not to exceed 1 allowance—see instructions on page 1) . . . . ▶ | B |
C   Allowances for dependents . . . . ▶ | C |

If you are not claiming any deductions or credits or income averaging, skip lines D and E.

D   Allowances for estimated deductions:

1   Enter the total amount of your estimated itemized deductions, alimony payments, qualified
    retirement contributions including IRA and Keogh (H.R. 10) plans, deduction for a married couple
    when both work, business losses including net operating loss carryovers, moving expenses,
    employee business expenses, penalty on early withdrawal of savings, and charitable contributions
    for nonitemizers for the year . . . . ▶ | 1 | $

2   If you do not plan to itemize deductions, enter $520 on line D2. If you plan to itemize, find your
    total estimated salaries and wages amount in the left column of the table below. (Include salaries
    and wages of both spouses.) Read across to the right and find the amount from the column that
    applies to you. Enter that amount on line D2. . . . . ▶ | 2 | $

Line D-1. Totaling Your Estimated Deductions

Extra withholding allowances are allowed for each $1,040 of your losses, excess itemized deductions, and adjustments (such as alimony payments, IRA payments, moving expenses) that exceed applicable Form W-4 Worksheet table amounts. (In most cases the table amounts are the zero bracket amount plus $520.)

IRS regulations allow you to consider just about every item that affects your tax liability when computing how many allowances you're entitled to claim. On the following pages you list each item to determine how it may affect the number of allowances you can claim.

First, there are a few IRS regulations you need to know:

- If you are also liable for making estimated tax payments, you must first use all the items of deductions, credits, and adjustments on the following pages to reduce your estimated tax liability before using them to offset your "wages" as additional withholding allowances. [IRS Reg. 31.3402(m)-1(b)]
- When estimating deductions, credits, losses, and adjustments, you must compute the aggregate dollar amount of a particular item that you reasonably expect will be allowed you for the estimation year. (The IRS says the estimation year is the taxable year that includes the day on which you give your employer a new W-4, unless you specifically mark it for next year. It's really just the year for which you are submitting your new W-4.)
- In no event should the estimated amount exceed the *sum* of the amount you deducted on last year's tax return *plus* any "determinable additional amounts," defined as amounts "that are demonstrably attributable to identifiable events during the estimation year or the preceding year." These are amounts that relate either to payments already made during the estimation year, to binding obligations to make payments during the year, or to other transactions or occurrences that have already begun and are verifiable. (What all this gobbledygook means is that

you can't claim more amounts on your W-4 Worksheet than you reasonably expect to be able to claim on your 1040 at the end of the year.)

Example: In January 1985 you obtained a divorce decree and were ordered by the court to pay $300 a month in alimony to your spouse. The alimony deduction is a "determinable additional amount" that is "demonstrably attributable to an identifiable event," and is also "verifiable."

Example: On July 18, 1984, you bought a house for the first time. You had never itemized before. Your mortgage interest and real estate taxes from July 18 through the end of the year are "determinable additional amounts" that also meet the other definitions.

Example: Your wife is pregnant and you expect to have extra medical bills due to the delivery. You cannot adjust your withholding allowances in anticipation of the expense. You must wait until the expenses have been incurred and become "determinable."

- If you have been audited for a previous tax year and a particular item was disallowed, the IRS will not allow you to use that item in your estimate for the estimation year for computing additional withholding allowances.

Summary of Your Estimated Deductions and Adjustments to Go on Line D-1 on Form W-4 Worksheet.

Write down on the next page your estimates for 1985. Use last year's tax return for help. If you are not sure whether particular items or expenses are deductible, check with the IRS or your favorite tax preparation guide.

Remember to include new obligations you will have to pay that you may not have had during the previous year—including alimony, mortgage, and IRA contributions.

- Itemized deductions (Schedule A, Line 24) ...... $_____
- Charitable contributions (for nonitemizers) ...... $_____
- Moving Expenses (Form 3903) .... $_____
- Deduction for married couple
  when both work (Schedule W) .... $_____
- Losses from Schedules C, D, E, F, and
  Form 4797 (last line, Part I) .... $_____
- Net operating loss carry-over
  from previous years .... $_____
- Estimated deduction for penalty on
  an early withdrawal of savings .... $_____
- Alimony payments you make .... $_____
- Qualified retirement contributions,
  including IRAs, and SEPs .... $_____
- Payments to self-employed retirement plan ...... $_____
- Employee business expenses
  (Part 1 of Form 2106) .... $_____

TOTAL OF DEDUCTIONS AND ADJUSTMENTS . $_____

STOP! *Before entering the above amount on Line D-1 of the Form W-4 Worksheet, you need to be aware of this IRS caution:*

Before you claim allowances under [lines] D and E, total your *nonwage* taxable income (interest, dividends, self-employment income, etc.) and subtract this amount from estimated deductions you would otherwise enter in D-1. If your nonwage income is greater than the amount of estimated deductions, you cannot claim any allowances under D.

Add, on the following lines, your estimated *nonwage* income for this year:

- Interest .... $_____
- Dividends in excess of exclusion
  (exclusion is $100 per spouse) .... $_____
- Refunds of state and local income
  taxes (from worksheet in 1040
  instruction booklet) .... $_____
- Alimony (received, not paid out) .... $_____
- Business income (losses are used
  in computing deductions for with-
  holding allowance computation above) .... $_____
- Capital gains (losses computed
  in above) .... $_____
- 40 percent capital gain distributions .... $_____
- Gains from Form 4797, "Supplemental
  Schedule of Gains and Losses" .... $_____
- Income from taxable pensions, annuities,
  etc., only if no tax is being withheld .... $_____
- Rents, royalties, partnerships,
  estates, trusts, etc. (from Schedule E,
  "Supplemental Income Schedule") .... $_____
- Farm income (from Schedule F) .... $_____
- Taxable amount of unemployment
  compensation (see worksheet in
  Form 1040 instruction booklet) .... $_____
- Other taxable income on which there
  is no tax withholding .... $_____

TOTAL OF NONWAGE INCOME .... $_____

Question: Is your total nonwage income greater than the estimated deductions you completed on page 37?

YES ☐   NO ☐

If your nonwage income is greater than the amount of your estimated deductions, you cannot claim any allowances under Line D. Go directly to the instructions for Line E. The total of your nonwage income will be used later, in Chapter 3, to determine if you should either reduce your withholding allowances or increase your withholding by specific amounts so that you will be sufficiently withheld and not be required to file and pay quarterly estimates on your nonwage income.

ENTER: Total of Estimated Deductions .... $_____
SUBTRACT: Total of Nonwage Income .... − $_____
RESULT: Amount to be entered on Line D-1 .... $_____

☐ If the total of your nonwage income is less than the amount of your estimated deductions computed on page 37, enter the amount of the difference (computed above) on Line D-1 of the Form W-4 Worksheet on page 30. Check this box when you have done this.

Line D-2. Computing Table Subtraction Amount

The first step for Line D-2 is to determine if you are going to itemize your deductions on Schedule A of your 1040. You can itemize only when your total number of Schedule A itemized deductions exceeds the following amounts for these filing statuses:

- Single, or head of household—$2,390 for 1985.
- Married filing jointly, or qualifying widow(er) with dependent child—$3,540 for 1985.
- Married filing separately—$1,770 for 1985.

☐ *If you are not going to itemize your deductions* on Schedule A this year, enter $520 on Line D-2 of the W-4 Worksheet on page 30, and check this box when you have done so. Now go to the instructions for Line D-3.

If you are going to itemize your deductions, use the table below to find the amount that will go on Line D-2. Find your total estimated salaries and wages (of both spouses if married, and from all sources) in the left-hand column. Then read across to the right and find the amount from the column that applies to you.

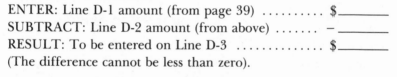

| 2 | If you do not plan to itemize deductions, enter $520 on line D2. If you plan to itemize, find your total estimated salaries and wages amount in the left column of the table below. (Include salaries and wages of both spouses.) Read across to the right and find the amount from the column that applies to you. Enter that amount on line D2. | | | | 2 | $ |

Estimated salaries and wages from all sources:	Single and Head of Household Employees (only one job)		Married Employees (one spouse working and one job only)		Employees with more than one job or Married Employees with both spouses working	
Under $20,000	. . $2,800		. . . $3,900		. . . 35%	
20,000-45,000	. . 2,800		. . . 3,900		. . . 22%	of estimated salaries and wages
45,001-60,000	. . 8%	of estimated salaries and wages	. . . 3,900		. . . 19%	
Over $60,000	. . 10%		. . . 7%	of estimated salaries and wages	. . . 18%	

Write here the amount to be entered on Line D-2: $_____ .

☐ Enter the above amount on Line D-2 of the Form W-4 Worksheet on page 30. Check this box when you have made that entry.

Line D-3. Remainder

ENTER: Line D-1 amount (from page 39) . . . . $_____
SUBTRACT: Line D-2 amount (from above) . . . . − _____
RESULT: To be entered on Line D-3 . . . . $_____
(The difference cannot be less than zero).

☐ Enter the above amount on Line D-3 of the Form W-4 Worksheet on page 30, and then check the box.

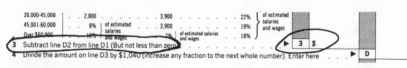

20,000-45,000	. . 2,800		. . . 3,900		. . . 22%	of estimated salaries and wages
45,001-60,000	. . 8%	of estimated salaries and wages	. . . 3,900		. . . 19%	
Over $60,000	. . 10%		. . . 7%	of estimated salaries and wages	. . . 18%	
3	Subtract line D2 from line D1 (But not less than zero). . . . . ▶ 3 $					
4	Divide the amount on line D3 by $1,040 (increase any fraction to the next whole number). Enter here . . . ▶ D					

LINE D-4. Computation of Withholding Allowances for Estimated Deductions

Divide the amount on Line D-3 by $1,040 and increase any fraction to the next whole number.

Example:

ENTER: Total estimated deductions from Line D-1 .. $15,000

SUBTRACT: Line D-2 amount ($42,000 in combined
salaries) ....   –   9,240

RESULT: Line D-3 equals .... $ 5,760

DIVIDE: Line D-3 amount by $1,040 ....   ÷ $ 1,040

RESULT EQUALS 5.54

ROUND: To next whole number ....   =   6

Thus withholding allowances go on Line D.

20,000-45,000	. . 2,800	 3,900	. . . . 22%	of estimated salaries and wages	
45,001-60,000	. . 8%	of estimated salaries and wages . . . 3,900	. . . . 19%		
Over $60,000	. . 10%	. . . 7%	of estimated salaries . . 18%	▶ 3 $	

3 Subtract line D2 from line D1 (But not less than zero) . . . .

4 Divide the amount on line D3 by $1,040 (increase any fraction to the next whole number). Enter here . . ▶ D

E Allowances for tax credits and income averaging: use Table 1 above for figuring withholding allowances

Make your computations here:

ENTER: Total estimated deductions from Line D-1 ..   _____

SUBTRACT: Line D-2 amount from table ....   – _____

RESULT: Line D-3 (but not less than zero) ....   = _____

DIVIDE: Line D-3 amount by $1,040 ....   ÷ $ 1,040

RESULT EQUALS ....   = _____

ROUND: To next whole number ....   _____

☐ Enter the number of withholding allowances you just computed for your estimated deductions on Line D of the Form W-4 Worksheet on page 30. Check this box when you have done so.

LINE E. ALLOWANCES FOR TAX CREDITS AND INCOME AVERAGING

Skip this section if you have no tax credits or don't expect to income average this year, and proceed to the instructions for Line F on page 49.

Line E-1. Computing the Credit Amounts

If you expect to have any tax credits (such as child and dependent care expenses, residential energy credit, political contributions credit) this year, or if you expect to income average, you may want to compute the additional withholding allowances you are entitled to claim to further reduce the amount of your tax being withheld.

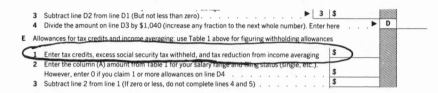

Because tax credits are a direct *subtraction* from your tax liability, and income averaging is a direct *reduction* in your tax liability, these items must be computed separately from the method used to compute your estimated deductions. Line E of the Form W-4 Worksheet and Table 1 that accompanies it (on the reverse side of the W-4, just above the Worksheet) will tell you how many allowances you are entitled to claim based on your expected tax credits and savings from income averaging.

Listed below are the items that can be added together to figure your additional allowances on Line E. Write the amount of your estimate on the appropriate line. The tax credit listings are divided into nonbusiness and business credits. If you are not in business for yourself, feel free to skip the business section.

Example: Nonbusiness tax credit situation

Paul and Laurie are both employed, with combined earnings and an adjusted gross income of $25,250. Paul earns $15,250 and Laurie earns $10,000. This year they estimate their child-care expenses at $5,000 for their two children (tax credit of $1,056), and they have spent $825 on new storm windows and doors that qualify for the residential energy credit (tax credit of $124). They also made a political contribution and expect some savings from income averaging. Their summary of tax credit items is:

- Credit for political contributions .... $ 100
- Credit for child care .... $ 1,056
- Residential energy credit .... $ 124
- Income averaging savings .... $ <u>144</u>

    TOTAL tax credit to be entered on Line E-1 ...... $ 1,424

E Allowances for tax credits and income averaging: use Table 1 above for figuring withholding allowances

1 Enter tax credits, excess social security tax withheld, and tax reduction from income averaging $*1,424*
2 Enter the column (A) amount from Table 1 for your salary range and filing status (single, etc.).
   However, enter 0 if you claim 1 or more allowances on line D4 . . . . $
3 Subtract line 2 from line 1 (If zero or less, do not complete lines 4 and 5) . . . . $
4 Find the column (B) amount from Table 1 for your salary range and filing status . . . . . . $
5 Divide line 3 by line 4. Increase any fraction to the next whole number. This is the maximum number of
   withholding allowances for tax credits and income averaging. Enter here . . . . ▶ **E**

Summary of your nonbusiness tax credits:

- Credit for the elderly and disabled .... $————
- Credit for political contributions .... $————
- Credit for child and disabled dependent care .... $————
- Residential energy credit .... $————
- Earned income credit .... $————
- Excess social security and railroad retirement
  withholding .... $————
- Savings from income averaging .... $————

    TOTAL nonbusiness tax credits .... $————

☐ Enter your total *nonbusiness tax credits* on Line E-1 of the Form W-4 Worksheet on page 30 *only if you* you have *no* business-related tax credits. Then skip the next section and proceed to the instructions for Line E-2 on the following page. Check this box if you are making an entry on Line E-1.

Summary of your business-related tax credits

- Foreign tax credit .... $_____

- Investment credit .... +_____

- Jobs credit .... +_____

- Alcohol fuel credit .... +_____

- Credit for federal tax on gasoline and
  special fuels .... +_____

- Credit for fuel from a nonconventional source .. +_____

- Research credit .... +_____

  TOTAL *Business-related Tax Credits* .... $_____

  ADD: Your *Nonbusiness Tax Credits* from above .. +_____

  TOTAL TAX CREDITS TO BE ENTERED
  ON LINE E-1 OF FORM W-4
  WORKSHEET ON PAGE 30 .... $_____

☐ Enter the above total of tax credits on Line E-1 of Form W-4 Worksheet on page 30, and then check this box.

Line E-2. Using Table 1, Column A, for Figuring Your Withholding Allowances for Credits and Income Averaging

☐ *Caution:* If you computed additional withholding allowances for your estimated deductions, and you are claiming one or more allowances on Line D-4 for those additional allowances, you should skip these instructions for Line E-2, enter "0" on Line E-2, and proceed to the instructions for Line E-3. Check the box if you are entering "0" on Line E-2.

Table 1 is used to compute the number of additional withholding allowances you are entitled to claim due to your tax credits and income averaging.

Table 1—For Figuring Your Withholding Allowances for Estimated Tax Credits and Income Averaging (Line E)

Estimated Salaries and Wages from All Sources	Single Employees		Head of Household Employees		Married Employees (When Spouse not Employed)		Married Employees (When Both Spouses Are Employed)	
	(A)	(B)	(A)	(B)	(A)	(B)	(A)	(B)
Under $15,000	90	$160	$ 0	$160	$ 50	$130	$ 0	$130
15,000-25,000	120	260	0	260	60	180	310	180
25,001-35,000	160	320	0	320	150	240	770	230
35,001-45,000	240	390	0	390	200	300	1,380	260
45,001-55,000	610	390	0	390	200	350	2,100	320
55,001-65,000	1,260	390	110	390	300	390	2,890	350
Over 65,000	2,250	390	730	390	570	390	3,590	390

To use the table, you must first find your estimated salaries and wages from all sources in the left-hand column and go across the table to the column for your current filing status or marital employment situation. Then use the figure under subcolumn (A) to enter on Line E-2.

Example

Combined earnings for Paul and Laurie are $25,250 per year. Since they are both working, they will go across the table to the last column, labeled "Married Employees (When Both Spouses are Employed)." The applicable value in subcolumn (A) is $770. This is the amount to enter on Line E-2.

Table 1—For Figuring Your Withholding Allowances for Estimated Tax Credits and Income Averaging (Line E)

Estimated Salaries and Wages from All Sources	Single Employees		Head of Household Employees		Married Employees (When Spouse not Employed)		Married Employees (When Both Spouses Are Employed)	
	(A)	(B)	(A)	(B)	(A)	(B)	(A)	(B)
Under $15,000	$ 90	$160	$ 0	$160	$ 50	$130	$ 0	$130
15,000-25,000	120	260	0	260	60	180	310	180
25,001-35,000	160	320	0	320	150	240	770	230
35,001-45,000	240	390	0	390	200	300	1,380	260
45,001-55,000	610	390	0	390	200	350	2,100	320
55,001-65,000	1,260	390	110	390	300	390	2,890	350
Over 65,000	2,250	390	730	390	570	390	3,590	390

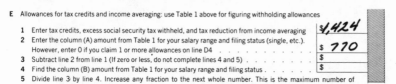

E Allowances for tax credits and income averaging: use Table 1 above for figuring withholding allowances

1 Enter tax credits, excess social security tax withheld, and tax reduction from income averaging $1,424
2 Enter the column (A) amount from Table 1 for your salary range and filing status (single, etc.).
  However, enter 0 if you claim 1 or more allowances on line D4 . . . . $ 770
3 Subtract line 2 from line 1 (If zero or less, do not complete lines 4 and 5) . . . . $
4 Find the column (B) amount from Table 1 for your salary range and filing status . . . . . . $
5 Divide line 3 by line 4. Increase any fraction to the next whole number. This is the maximum number of

Caution: *If on page 38 you determined that your nonwage income was greater than your total of estimated deductions, you need to make an adjustment for subcolumn (A). Compute here the amount that your nonwage income exceeds your estimated deductions on page 37.*

Example

ENTER: Amount of nonwage income	$15,000
SUBTRACT: Amount of estimated deductions and adjustments	−$10,000
RESULT: Excess of nonwage income	=$ 5,000
DIVIDE: Excess by 3	÷ 3
RESULT EQUALS	$ 1,667
ADD: The appropriate (A) value from Table 1	+$ 2,100
TOTAL: Amount to go on Line E-2	$ 3,767

Make your computations here:

ENTER: Amount of nonwage income .... $_____

SUBTRACT: Amount of estimated deductions and
adjustments ....   − _____

RESULT: Excess of nonwage income ....   = _____

DIVIDE: Excess by 3 ....   ÷   3

RESULT EQUALS ....   _____

ADD: The appropriate (A) value from Table 1 .... +   _____

TOTAL: Amount to go on Line E-2 ....   =   _____

☐ If you have made a computation here, check this box after you have entered the above amount on Line E-2 of the W-4 Worksheet on page 30.

INSTRUCTION:

If the above section did not apply to you, and the above box was not checked, you should now go to the appropriate subcolumn (A) value for your income level, filing status, or marital situation, and write that amount here: $_____ .

☐ Enter the above amount on Line E-2 of the W-4 Worksheet on page 30 and check this box when you have done so.

Now proceed with the instructions for Line E-3.

Line E-3. Subtraction Result

Example for Paul and Laurie

E Allowances for tax credits and income averaging: use Table 1 above for figuring withholding allowances

1 Enter tax credits, excess social security tax withheld, and tax reduction from income averaging $ *1,424*
2 Enter the column (A) amount from Table 1 for your salary range and filing status (single, etc.).
   However, enter 0 if you claim 1 or more allowances on line D4 . . . . $ *770*
3 Subtract line 2 from line 1 (If zero or less, do not complete lines 4 and 5) . . . . $ *654*
4 Find the column (B) amount from Table 1 for your salary range and filing status . . . . . . $
5 Divide line 3 by line 4. Increase any fraction to the next whole number. This is the maximum number of
   withholding allowances for tax credits and income averaging. Enter here . . . .   ▶ | E

ENTER: Amount from Line E-1 . . . . $_____
SUBTRACT: Amount from Line E-2 . . . . − _____
RESULT: To go on Line E-3 . . . . = _____

☐ Enter the above result on Line E-3 of the Form W-4 Worksheet on page 30 and check this box when you have done that.

Note: If the amount on Line E-3 is zero or less, do not complete Lines E-4 and E-5. This means that your tax credit and income averaging amounts do not exceed the IRS's table values, and therefore you have no additional withholding allowances for these items.

Line E-4. Using Column (B)

Look at Table 1 (repeated on page 48) and find the line in the left-hand column that approximates your combined estimated salaries and wages for the year. Then go across the table to the column for your filing status or marital situation. This time find the appropriate value in column (B).

Table 1—For Figuring Your Withholding Allowances for Estimated Tax Credits and Income Averaging (Line E)

Estimated Salaries and Wages from All Sources	Single Employees		Head of Household Employees		Married Employees (When Spouse not Employed)		Married Employees (When Both Spouses Are Employed)	
	(A)	(B)	(A)	(B)	(A)	(B)	(A)	(B)
Under $15,000	$ 90	$160	$ 0	$160	$ 50	$130	$ 0	$130
15,000-25,000	120	260	0	260	60	180	310	180
25,001-35,000	160	320	0	320	150	240	770	230
35,001-45,000	240	390	0	390	200	300	1,380	260
45,001-55,000	610	390	0	390	200	350	2,100	320
55,001-65,000	1,260	390	110	390	300	390	2,890	350
Over 65,000	2,250	390	730	390	570	390	3,590	390

Example for Paul and Laurie

E Allowances for tax credits and income averaging: use Table 1 above for figuring withholding allowances

1 Enter tax credits, excess social security tax withheld, and tax reduction from income averaging $*1,424*
2 Enter the column (A) amount from Table 1 for your salary range and filing status (single, etc.).
   However, enter 0 if you claim 1 or more allowances on line D4 . . . . $ *770*
3 Subtract line 2 from line 1 (If zero or less, do not complete lines 4 and 5) . . . . $ *654*
4 Find the column (B) amount from Table 1 for your salary range and filing status . . . . . . $ *230*
5 Divide line 3 by line 4. Increase any fraction to the next whole number. This is the maximum number of
   withholding allowances for tax credits and income averaging. Enter here . . . . ▶ **E**

Write here the amount to be entered on Line E-4: $_____

☐ Enter the appropriate subcolumn (B) amount on Line E-4 of the Form W-4 Worksheet on page 30. Check this box when you have done so.

Line E-5. Computing the Number of Allowances

Example for Laurie and Paul

E Allowances for tax credits and income averaging: use Table 1 above for figuring withholding allowances

1 Enter tax credits, excess social security tax withheld, and tax reduction from income averaging $*1,424*
2 Enter the column (A) amount from Table 1 for your salary range and filing status (single, etc.).
   However, enter 0 if you claim 1 or more allowances on line D4 . . . . $ *770*
3 Subtract line 2 from line 1 (If zero or less, do not complete lines 4 and 5) . . . . $ *654*
4 Find the column (B) amount from Table 1 for your salary range and filing status . . . . . . $ *230*
5 Divide line 3 by line 4. Increase any fraction to the next whole number. This is the maximum number of
   withholding allowances for tax credits and income averaging. Enter here . . . . ▶ **E** *3*

ENTER: Amount from Line E-3 .... _____

DIVIDE: By Line E-4 amount .... ÷ _____

RESULT EQUALS .... _____

ROUND: To the next whole number .... _____

This is the maximum number of withholding allowances you are entitled to claim for your tax credits and income averaging.

☐ Enter the number of withholding allowances you have just computed for your tax credits and income averaging on Line E of your Form W-4 Worksheet on page 30. Check this box when you have done so.

LINE F. TOTAL WORKSHEET ALLOWANCES

At this point you have computed all the withholding allowances you are legally entitled to claim, and the final computation is to add the following:

ENTER: Line A   Personal Allowances ....   _____

ADD: Line B   Special Withholding Allowance .. + _____

ADD: Line C   Allowances for Dependents ..... + _____

ADD: Line D   Allowances for Estimated
                 Deductions .... + _____

ADD: Line E   Allowances for Tax Credits and
                 Income Averaging .... + _____

EQUALS total number of Withholding Allowances on
    Line F: .... _____

☐ Enter the above total on Line F of the Form W-4 Worksheet on page 30. Check this box when you have done so.

You have just computed all the withholding allowances you are legally entitled to claim. To ensure that you do not become underwithheld, proceed to Chapter 3. Do not make an entry on the front side of your W-4 until you have verified the number of allowances computed above by reading Chapter 3 and completing the Worksheet at the end of that chapter.

CHAPTER THREE

Adjusting Your Withholding Allowances to Meet Your Total Tax Liability

In Chapter 2 you learned how to compute the maximum number of withholding allowances that you are legally entitled to claim. In this chapter you will learn to estimate your tax liability and compare it with your total withholding, to prevent underwithholding.

Your maximum withholding allowances are determined solely by the amount of your deductions, exemptions, tax credits, adjustments, and Schedule G (income averaging) savings. The number of allowances that you should claim, however, is related to your total income from all sources and thus to your total tax liability.

Adjusting your withholding, after you have calculated your maximum withholding allowances, is essential:
  - *If you have additional nonwage sources of income.*
  - *If you are married and there are at least two jobs between you and your spouse.*

If you have additional income, such as interest, dividends, alimony and capital gains, you need to make sure that you are not going to be *underwithheld* by claiming all the allowances you are legally entitled to claim. This is particularly important if your non-wage income exceeds your estimated deductions.

The withholding tables do not contain an adjustment factor for nonwage income. On the contrary, the withholding tables assume that you *do not have* additional sources of income, by virtue of the fact that the number of allowances you claim with your employer will result in tax withholding that reflects *solely that income* earned at an annual rate.

If you have several thousands of dollars in extra nonwage income, you could very well end up owing the IRS if *you* don't make the necessary adjustment. On the other hand, you don't want to overreact to the possibility of being underwithheld by deliberately overwithholding. Your objective should be to match your withholding to your tax liability, and increase your net paycheck.

Remember that you have a legal responsibility to be properly withheld, but that you have no legal responsibility to lend part of your paycheck every payday to Uncle Sam.

If you have extra nonwage income, you need to be aware of the requirements for filing estimated tax payments. Estimated tax is the amount of tax you expect to owe for the year after subtracting the amount of tax you expect to have withheld and the amount of any credits you plan to take. *But you're not required to make estimated tax payments if* your income tax return at the end of the year will show a refund or a balance due of less than $500 (beginning in 1985).

You must make estimated payments if your estimated tax balance due is $500 or more *and* if either (1) or (2), below, applies to you. You expect your 1985 gross income:

1. To include more than $500 from sources other than wages subject to withholding; *or*
2. To be more than:
   —$20,000 if you are single, a head of household, or a qualifying widow or widower;
   —$20,000 if you are married, can make joint estimated tax payments, and your spouse has not received wages for 1985;
   —$10,000 if you are married, can make joint estimated tax payments, and both of you have received wages for 1985;
   —$5,000 if you are married but cannot make joint estimated tax payments. (No joint estimated tax payments may be made if either you or your spouse is a nonresident alien, you are separated under a decree of divorce or separate maintenance, or you have different tax years.)

If you are a wage earner or a salaried employee, you can avoid having to make estimated tax payments by reducing your number of withholding allowances or asking your employer to take more tax out of your earnings. All you have to do, in either case, is file a new W-4 Certificate with your employer.

Important: *If you are a wage earner or a salaried employee and your nonwage income causes you to meet the requirements to make estimated tax payments, you can increase your withholding sufficiently to avoid having to make the estimated tax payments.*

The IRS will allow you not to file the estimated tax payments if you have a sufficient amount of withholding to cover your additional taxes due to your nonwage income. Filing 1040-ES vouchers every quarter to make estimated tax payments when it is not necessary is a waste of time and energy. In addition, if you're not used to making quarterly estimated tax payments you run the risk of forgetting to make them, and thus being underwithheld at the end of the year.

If you are entitled to claim a lot of allowances, you will probably be able to meet your additional tax liability due to nonwage income by reducing your allowances accordingly. (Remember the adjustment you made in Chapter 2 where you reduced your estimated deductions and adjustments by the amount of your nonwage income?) Even if you find that reducing down to zero allowances is insufficient, you can ask your employer to withhold additional amounts. Just compute how much additional tax you'll owe, divide it by the number of pay periods in the year, and put that amount on Line 5 of your W-4 Certificate.

---

4 Total number of allowances you are claiming (from line F of the worksheet on page 2) . . . .
5 Additional amount, if any, you want deducted from each pay . . . . $

6 claim exemption from withholding because (see instructions) and check boxes below that apply):
a ☐ Last year I did not owe any Federal income tax and had a right to a full refund of **ALL** income tax withheld, **AND**
b ☐ This year I do not expect to owe any Federal income tax and expect to have a right to a full refund of   Year
   ALL income tax withheld. If both a and b apply, enter the year effective and "EXEMPT" here . . ▶

Example

Linda is single and only entitled to two allowances—one for herself and one for the special withholding allowance. Her salary is $30,000 a year, and last year she had $4,000 in interest from a large savings account, $1,200 in taxable dividends, and $3,000 in long-term capital gains (of which 40 percent, or $1,200, is taxable). Her tax liability last year was $7,167, but her withholding was only $6,453.60. This was $537.80 per monthly pay period on a monthly income of $2,500 with zero allowances. Since Linda was under-withheld by $713.40 in 1984 and expects to have the same tax liability in 1985, she filed a new W-4 Certificate with her employer, and asked him to withhold an additional $59.45 per month ($713.40 ÷ 12 = $59.45). This will bring her tax withholding up to par with her estimated tax liability.

ESTIMATING YOUR EXPECTED TAX LIABILITY

The only way to determine if your adjusted withholding is going to work for you is by comparing the estimated amount of income tax to be withheld for the year to an estimate of your expected tax liability.

To help you adjust your withholding properly we have included the IRS income tax withholding tables in this book (see Appendix 1). These tables are current through December 31, 1985, and represent the most common method of computing income tax withholding. All you have to do is turn to your chart for your marital status and payroll period, find the column that corresponds to your wages, and proceed across the page to the figure that lies under the number of withholding allowances you are claiming to find the amount of income tax to withhold.

You can also use these charts to gauge whether your employer is withholding the correct amount as specified on your W-4 Certificate. But don't be surprised if the amount of actual tax withheld varies a little from the figure shown in the chart. There are several methods your employer can use to determine how much tax to withhold, and each may produce a slightly different amount.

To compute how much your withheld tax will equal or exceed your expected tax liability, you need to utilize a Form 1040, the withholding tables in Appendix 1, and the tax rate schedules in Appendix 2. You also need to put together the following information (write the proper figures on the applicable lines):

- Your annual income (from all sources, and
  from both spouses if filing jointly) .... $_____
- Your marital status for tax purposes .... _____
- The maximum number of withholding allowances
  you're legally entitled to claim (see Chapter 2) ..... _____
- Your gross income at each paycheck .... $_____
- The frequency of each paycheck (i.e.,
  weekly, monthly, etc.) .... _____

The IRS says that in some cases claiming all the withholding allowances to which you are entitled *may* result in your being under-withheld. This is particularly likely if you are married and both you and your spouse work. But there is a process that you can use to determine if the adjustment to your tax withholding will create a problem for you. If there is a large difference between the amount of tax being withheld and your expected tax liability, then further computations and adjustments may have to be made.

If you find that by claiming more allowances (and up to the maximum number) you are still overwithheld, then you're just going to have to accept it. The law does not allow you to claim more allowances than you're entitled to claim. However, the withholding tables are so constructed that if you claim the maximum permissible number of allowances, your overwithholding (if any) should be at a minimum. On the other hand, if claiming more allowances creates a situation of being underwithheld, you may need to cut back on your allowances to a lower number that will solve the under-withholding problem.

To determine how well your withholding will approximate your expected tax liability you should follow these steps:

STEP 1

Compute all the withholding allowances to which you are legally entitled on a W-4 Worksheet.

STEP 2

Go to the withholding tables in Appendix 1 and find out how much income tax will be withheld from your paycheck based on your marital status, income, and pay period, and the number of withholding allowances you are entitled to claim.

STEP 3

Multiply the amount of income tax withheld per paycheck by the number of pay periods per year to compute the total amount of income tax that will be withheld for the year.

STEP 4

Compute what your expected tax liability will be for the current year by considering all sources of income, the total number of allowances you will claim from exemptions, tax credits, and itemized deductions. Use the tax rate schedules in Appendix 2 of this book to estimate your expected tax liability for 1985.

STEP 5

Subtract from your expected tax liability, which you've just computed, the total amount of income tax to be withheld for the year to determine whether there is underwithholding or overwithholding.

STEP 6

Decide whether you are underwithheld or overwithheld, and then what to do. If your withholding (Step 3) exceeds your expected tax liability slightly, then you're in great shape. If your withholding falls short of your expected tax liability, then you need to decide if you want to be underwithheld.

The two primary considerations are whether you will be penalized and whether you will have the money next April 15. If 80 percent or more of your tax liability is being paid through withholding and/or estimated tax payments, then no penalty will be assessed for being underwithheld.

The next decision is to determine if owing money to the IRS will present a financial problem for you. If you decide that claiming all the withholding allowances to which you're entitled will present a problem to you, because of the possibility of having to pay more, then you should claim fewer allowances. The withholding tables in

Appendix 1 will enable you to determine which number of allowances should be claimed to prevent being underwithheld.

Before you begin, study the following examples, which will help you understand the methodology involved in determining whether or not your adjustment to Form W-4 will create a possible problem of being underwithheld.

Example 1

Stanley is single, and earns $32,500 a year, or $1,250 per biweekly pay period. Because of $3,000 in itemized deductions, a $2,000 IRA payment, and $3,000 in carry-over losses from last year's Schedule D, Stanley computes that he's entitled to seven allowances: one personal, one special, and five on Line D of the W-4 Worksheet.

STEP 1
Compute the number of allowances you're legally
entitled to claim (from Chapter 2)   7

STEP 2
Go to the withholding tables and find how much will
be withheld per payroll period .... $ 186.00

STEP 3
Multiply the amount in Step 2 by number of pay
periods in year (26): .... ×   26
Total amount of withholding for the year .... $ 4,836

STEP 4
Compute your expected tax liability, using this formula:
Total income (Line 23 of Form 1040) .... $ 29,500
Subtract adjustments to income .... −   2,000
Equals adjusted gross income .... $ 27,500
Subtract excess itemized deductions .... −   610
(Line 26 of Schedule A—Itemized Deductions)

```
Equals ....................................... $   26,890
Subtract exemptions ($1,040 each) ............ -    1,040
Equals taxable income ....................... $   25,850
Tax liability ................................ $ 4,700.70
Subtract tax credits ......................... -        0
Equals ....................................... $ 4,700.70
Add other taxes .............................. +        0

Total tax liability .......................... $ 4,700.70
```

STEP 5

```
Enter your expected tax liability ................ $ 4,700.70
Subtract amount to be withheld in Step 3 ........ - 4,836.00
                                                   $ - 135.30
```

STEP 6

Decide if you are underwithheld, or overwithheld. (Negative result in Step 5 means overwithheld; positive result, underwithheld.)

In this example Stanley has computed all the withholding allowances he's allowed to carry, and he's overwithheld by $135.30. Stanley has taken all the withholding allowances he's legally entitled to claim, but will be overwithheld only a small amount.

Example 2

Roberta is single and earns $24,000 a year ($2,000 a month) as a police officer. Her nonwage income in 1984 was $900 in interest, $250 in dividends (before the $100 exclusion), and $2,800 in additional net income from the sales of crafts she made. She expects her income to be the same in 1985. She was underwithheld in 1984 and wants to break even for 1985.

STEP 1

```
Compute the number of allowances you're legally
entitled to claim (from Chapter 2) ...................    2
```

STEP 2

Go to the withholding tables and find how much will
be withheld per payroll period .... $ 330.00

STEP 3

Multiply amount in Step 2 by number of pay periods
in year (12): .... ×   12

Total amount of withholding for the year = ... $ 3,960.00

STEP 4

Compute your expected tax liability, using this formula:

Total income (Line 23 of Form 1040) .... $ 27,850

Subtract adjustments to income .... −   0

Equals adjusted gross income .... $ 27,850

Subtract excess itemized deductions .... −   0

(Line 26 of Schedule A—Itemized Deductions)

Equals .... $ 27,850

Subtract exemptions ($1,040 each) .... −   1,040

Equals taxable income .... $ 26,810

Tax liability .... $ 4,988.70

Subtract tax credits .... −   0

Equals .... $ 4,988.70

Add other taxes (self-employment) .... +   330.40

Total tax liability .... $ 5,319.10

STEP 5

Enter your expected tax liability .... $ 5,319.10

Subtract amount to be withheld in Step 3 .... − 3,960.00

+ $1,359.10

STEP 6

Decide if you are underwithheld, or overwithheld and what to
do. (Negative amount in Step 5 means overwithheld; positive
amount, underwithheld.)

If underwithheld,

Enter your expected tax liability .... $ 5,319.10
Subtract your spouse's withholding for the year .. − ___0___
Equals your necessary withholding .... $ 5,319.10

Divide your necessary withholding from above
by the number of your payroll periods .... ÷ ___12___

Equals your necessary withholding per payroll
period .... $ __443.26__

Go to proper wage bracket withholding table for
salary/wage income of *$2,000 per month* and find
smallest number of allowances closest to but
slightly over above amount .... ___0___

If answer is zero, go to Step 7.

STEP 7

Enter amount of necessary withholding
per pay period .... $ 443.26
Subtract amount at zero allowances .... − __377.00__

Equals amount of extra withholding needed
each pay period .... $ __66.26__

Enter amount on Line 5 of W-4 Certificate as extra withholding.

In this example Roberta is underwithheld because she has additional nonwage income, such as interest, dividends, and business income, that has thrown her into a higher tax bracket. This example was used to show you what to do if you become underwithheld by claiming the number of allowances you're entitled to claim, and what you must do if claiming zero allowances doesn't solve your problem. Here Roberta must ask her employer to withhold an additional amount of tax from each paycheck, and she does this by entering $66.26 on Line 5 of her W-4 Certificate.

Example 3

Mike is 42 years old, married, has three little boys who are his dependents, and makes $650 a week (or $33,800 a year) as an engineer. His wife Joan is a nurse and makes $320 per week (or $16,640 per year). Since Mike is only claiming five allowances and Joan claims zero, they get large refunds every year. Mike always liked the idea of a forced savings, but a neighbor convinced him to reduce his withholding and send the extra "savings" to his credit union via allotment.

Mike's current withholding is $90.00 per paycheck, and Joan's is $39.00 per paycheck for a yearly total of $6,708. In computing how many withholding allowances he's entitled to claim, Mike uses the following information:

Income:
Mike's income ($650 per week) .... $ 33,800
Joan's income ($320 per week)   16,640
Interest income   1,400
Total income .... = $ 51,840

Adjustments to income:
Employee business expense .... $ 898
Deduction for working married couple   1,664
Total adjustments .... $ 2,562

Itemized deductions:
Total of itemized deductions .... $ 17,079
Subtract zero bracket amount .... −   3,540
   Schedule A, Line 26 (Excess Itemized Deductions) $ 13,539

Mike and Joan's W-4 Worksheet is shown on page 61.

Needless to say, Mike and Joan were a little worried when they computed *fifteen* withholding allowances for Mike. It occurred to them that claiming this many allowances might make them under-withheld, and they were worried because they knew that Mike's employer would have to send his W-2 to the IRS for review. (Actu-

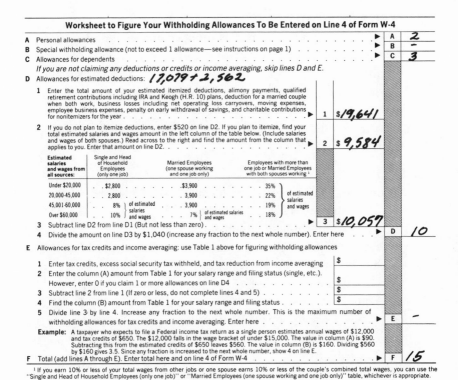

Worksheet to Figure Your Withholding Allowances To Be Entered on Line 4 of Form W-4

A Personal allowances . . . . ▶ **A** _2_

B Special withholding allowance (not to exceed 1 allowance—see instructions on page 1) . . . . ▶ **B** _—_

C Allowances for dependents . . . . ▶ **C** _3_

If you are not claiming any deductions or credits or income averaging, skip lines D and E.

D Allowances for estimated deductions: *17,079 + 2,562*

1 Enter the total amount of your estimated itemized deductions, alimony payments, qualified retirement contributions including IRA and Keogh (H.R. 10) plans, deduction for a married couple when both work, business losses including net operating loss carryovers, moving expenses, employee business expenses, penalty on early withdrawal of savings, and charitable contributions for nonitemizers for the year . . . . ▶ **1** $*19,641*

2 If you do not plan to itemize deductions, enter $520 on line D2. If you plan to itemize, find your total estimated salaries and wages amount in the left column of the table below. (Include salaries and wages of both spouses.) Read across to the right and find the amount from the column that applies to you. Enter that amount on line D2. . . . . ▶ **2** $ *9,584*

Estimated salaries and wages from all sources:	Single and Head of Household Employees (only one job)	Married Employees (one spouse working and one job only)	Employees with more than one job or Married Employees with both spouses working [1]
Under $20,000	. $2,800	. $3,900	. 35%
20,000-45,000	. 2,800	. 3,900	. 22% } of estimated salaries and wages
45,001-60,000	. 8% } of estimated salaries and wages	. 3,900	. 19%
Over $60,000	. 10% }	. 7% } of estimated salaries and wages	. 18%

3 Subtract line D2 from line D1 (But not less than zero). . . . . ▶ **3** $*10,057*

4 Divide the amount on line D3 by $1,040 (increase any fraction to the next whole number). Enter here . . . ▶ **D** _10_

E Allowances for tax credits and income averaging: use Table 1 above for figuring withholding allowances

1 Enter tax credits, excess social security tax withheld, and tax reduction from income averaging $____

2 Enter the column (A) amount from Table 1 for your salary range and filing status (single, etc.). However, enter 0 if you claim 1 or more allowances on line D4 $____

3 Subtract line 2 from line 1 (If zero or less, do not complete lines 4 and 5) . . . . $____

4 Find the column (B) amount from Table 1 for your salary range and filing status . . . . . . $____

5 Divide line 3 by line 4. Increase any fraction to the next whole number. This is the maximum number of withholding allowances for tax credits and income averaging. Enter here . . . . ▶ **E** _—_

Example: A taxpayer who expects to file a Federal income tax return as a single person estimates annual wages of $12,000 and tax credits of $650. The $12,000 falls in the wage bracket of under $15,000. The value in column (A) is $90. Subtracting this from the estimated credits of $650 leaves $560. The value in column (B) is $160. Dividing $560 by $160 gives 3.5. Since any fraction is increased to the next whole number, show 4 on line E.

F Total (add lines A through E). Enter total here and on line 4 of Form W-4 . . . . ▶ **F** _15_

[1] If you earn 10% or less of your total wages from other jobs or one spouse earns 10% or less of the couple's combined total wages, you can use the "Single and Head of Household Employees (only one job)" or "Married Employees (one spouse working and one job only)" table, whichever is appropriate.

ally, though, they shouldn't have worried about that. Being under-withheld is their only worry.)

Mike and Joan recomputed their allowances to take into account their estimated nonwage income, for which there is no withholding. This is their worksheet:

STEP 1

Compute the number of allowances you're legally entitled to claim (from Chapter 2)   15

STEP 2

Go to the withholding tables and find how much will be withheld per payroll period . . . . $ 44.14

STEP 3

Multiply amount in Step 2 by number of pay periods
in year (52): .... × ___52___

Equals .... $ 2,295.28
Add withholding of spouse if both work during the
year .... + 2,028.00

Total amount of withholding for the year .... $ 4,323.28

STEP 4

Compute your expected tax liability, using this formula:

Total income (Line 23 of Form 1040) .... $ 51,840
Subtract adjustments to income .... −   2,562

Equals adjusted gross income .... $ 49,278
Subtract excess itemized deductions .... − 13,539

(Line 26 of Schedule A—Itemized Deductions)
Equals .... $ 35,739
Subtract exemptions ($1,040 each) .... −   5,200

Equals taxable income .... $ 30,539
Tax liability .... $ 4,840.35
Subtract tax credits .... −   0

Equals .... $ 4,840.35
Add other taxes .... +   0

Total tax liability .... $ 4,840.35

STEP 5

Enter your expected tax liability .... $ 4,840.35
Subtract amount to be withheld in Step 3 .... − 4,323.28
Difference is .... $ 517.07

STEP 6

Decide if you are underwithheld or overwithheld and
what to do. (Negative amount in Step 5 is overwithheld;
positive amount, underwithheld.)

If underwithheld,

Enter your expected tax liability .... $ 4,840.35

Subtract your spouse's withholding for the year .. − 2,028.00

Equals your necessary withholding .... $ 2,812.35

Divide your necessary withholding from above by
the number of your payroll periods .... ÷   52

Equals your necessary withholding per payroll
period .... $ 54.08

Go to proper wage bracket withholding table for
salary/wage income of $650 *per week* and find smallest
number of allowances closest to but slightly over
above amount 10

If answer is 10 or over, go to Step 7.

STEP 7

Enter amount to be withheld at 10 allowances ..... $ 66.00

Subtract amount of necessary withholding per
payroll period .... −   54.08

Equals overwithholding at 10 allowances .... (A)   11.92

Enter amount to be withheld at 9 allowances 70.00

Subtract amount to be withheld at 10 allowances . −   66.00

Equals per 1 allowance withholding value .... (B)   4.00

Divide (A) amount by (B) amount ($11.92 ÷ 4.00) =   2.98

Add 10 allowances to above .... +   10.00

Equals number of allowances to claim
on Form W-4, Line 4 ....   12.98

(Drop any fraction to be slightly overwithheld, or
increase to next whole number to be slightly
underwithheld.) 13

By using the above worksheet, Mike and Joan recomputed their withholding allowances to *thirteen.* This adjustment was needed because of their nonwage income, their joint incomes, and their desire not to owe the IRS very much money at the end of the year.

Mike is interested in finding out how close the withholding from claiming thirteen allowances is to par with his expected tax liability. So Mike recomputes his withholding using the Percentage Method of Withholding Tables:

- 12 allowances = $55.64 per pay period withholding or $2,893.28 per year.
- 13 allowances = $51.24 per pay period withholding or $2,664.48 per year.

With twelve allowances, Mike will be overwithheld $80.93 (actual withholding of $2,893.28 less the necessary withholding of $2,812.35). With thirteen allowances, Mike will be underwithheld $147.87. In this example, Mike decides it is okay to be under-withheld $147.87.

In any event, Mike doesn't have to worry, because his withheld taxes are over 80 percent of his expected tax liability and if his tax liability does not increase, he will not get penalized, even if he claimed all fifteen allowances. Mike can claim any number of al-lowances at 15 or below. He cannot claim more than 15 allowances, the number computed on his W-4 Worksheet.

Remember, though, that the penalty for not making estimated tax payments is based on the difference between your total with-holding plus your estimated tax payments and the final tax liability computed and reported on your tax return.

YOUR WORKSHEET FOR ADJUSTING YOUR WITHHOLDING ALLOWANCES

On the next page begins the worksheet for adjusting your with-holding allowances. You should use this worksheet after you've computed the number of allowances you're legally entitled to claim in Chapter 2.

For this worksheet you will need to refer to the withholding tables for 1985 in Appendix 1 in the back of this book, and the Tax Rate Schedules for 1985 in Appendix 2.

If you're married and plan on filing a joint return, and have computed your allowances jointly, you may divide them up any way you wish. When using this worksheet, there are two approaches you can take:

(1) When you divide up the total number of allowances to which you are legally entitled, a decision should be made as to which spouse will keep that agreed upon number of allowances and which spouse will be subject to the adjustment, if any, by use of this worksheet. If you are the spouse whose withholding will be subject to adjustment, then you should enter the number of allowances you've initially agreed to claim in Step 1. Your spouse's withholding will be added in steps 3 and 6.

(2) The easiest approach is to decide that one spouse will claim zero allowances to begin with and the total number of allowances entered in Step 1 will be the combined number computed in Chapter 2. The withholding amounts of the spouse initially claiming zero allowances will be entered in steps 3 and 6. The worksheet will then compute the total number of allowances, as adjusted, for both spouses. Once the adjusted number of allowances has been computed, they can then be divided in any manner as agreed. However, best results will be obtained if the number of allowances finally claimed are exactly as computed in the worksheet with only one spouse making an adjustment to his/her withholding.

YOUR WORKSHEET FOR ADJUSTING YOUR WITHHOLDING ALLOWANCES

STEP 1
Compute the number of allowances you're legally
entitled to claim (from Chapter 2) .... ⎯⎯⎯⎯

STEP 2
Go to the withholding tables and find how much
will be withheld per payroll period .... $⎯⎯⎯⎯

STEP 3

Multiply amount in Step 2 by number of pay periods
in year: .... × _____

Equals .... _____

Add withholding of spouse if both work
during the year .... + _____

Total amount of withholding for the year .... _____

STEP 4

Compute your expected tax liability, using this formula:

Total 1985 income (Line 23 of Form 1040) .... _____

Subtract adjustments to income .... − _____

Equals adjusted gross income .... _____

Subtract excess itemized deductions .... − _____

  (Line 26 of Schedule A—Itemized Deductions)

Equals .... _____

Subtract exemptions ($1,040 each) .... − _____

Equals taxable income .... _____

Tax liability (Use Tax Rate Schedules in
Appendix 2) .... _____

Subtract tax credits .... − _____

Equals .... _____

Add other taxes .... + _____

Total tax liability .... $ _____

STEP 5

Enter your expected tax liability .... _____

Subtract the total amount to be withheld in Step 3 − _____

Difference is .... _____

STEP 6

Decide if you are underwithheld or overwithheld, and what to
do. (Negative amount in Step 5 is overwithheld; positive amount,
underwithheld.)

If *overwithheld* and you have claimed all the allowances you're
legally entitled to claim, you have done your best.

If *underwithheld*,

Enter your expected tax liability .... _____

Subtract your spouse's withholding for the year ... − _____

Equals your necessary withholding .... _____
Divide your necessary withholding from above by
the number of your payroll periods .... ÷ _____
Equals your necessary withholding per pay period .. _____
Go to proper wage bracket withholding table for
salary/wage income of $_____ per _____ (period)
and find smallest number of allowances closest but
slightly over above amount .... _____
If answer is zero, go to Step 7. If answer is 10 or over, go to Step 8.

STEP 7

Enter amount of necessary withholding per pay
period .... _____
Subtract amount at zero allowances .... − _____
Difference: Amount of extra withholding needed each
pay period .... _____
Enter amount above on Line 5 of W-4 Certificate (page 4) as
extra withholding.

STEP 8

Enter amount to be withheld at 10 allowances ...... _____
Subtract amount of necessary withholding per
payroll period .... − _____
Equals overwithholding at 10 allowances .... (A) _____
Enter amount to be withheld at 9 allowances .... _____
Subtract amount to be withheld at 10 allowances .. − _____
Equals per one allowance withholding value ..... (B)_____
Divide (A) amount by (B) amount
                  _____ ÷ _____ .... = _____
Add 10 allowances to above .... + ___10___
Equals number of allowances to claim on Form W-4,
Line 4 .... _____

Note: Drop any fraction if you want to be slightly overwithheld, or increase to next whole number to be slightly
underwithheld.

Enter number of allowances to claim here
and on Form W-4, Line 4 .... _____

CHAPTER FOUR

Buying a Personal Residence for the First Time, or Significantly Increasing Your Mortgage Payments

---

Read this chapter if you:
- *Recently bought a home, house or residential condominium for the first time.*
- *Recently increased your mortgage interest and real estate taxes significantly either because of a purchase, a refinancing, or a second mortgage.*

If you are a first-time home buyer, you are most likely a 1040A filer who has never itemized deductions. Your home purchase will probably cause you to itemize for the first time, and, most likely, your real estate agent has already counseled you on the tax benefits of buying a house. And, most likely, your real estate agent has told you that you don't have to wait until next year before availing yourself of these benefits. But it is most unlikely that your real estate agent shoved a new W-4 in your hands and helped you compute how to adjust your withholding allowances to maximize the benefits of your new tax shelter.

Even if your agent did help you compute your new additional withholding allowances to increase your paycheck and take your tax benefits "up front," it is highly unlikely that he or she showed you IRS's "new" computational method, which can only be used in computing additional withholding allowances where there are increases in mortgage interest and real estate taxes due to a purchase or ownership of real property.

If you are an experienced home owner, you are well aware of the benefits of using your home as a tax shelter by deducting your mortgage interest and real estate taxes on your tax return. And if you have just recently sold your home to purchase a new one (new to you, that is), you probably incurred a bigger mortgage expense with corresponding higher real estate taxes. In the last couple of years it has not been uncommon for people to burden themselves with mortgages over 12 percent, a phenomenon unheard of in the 1970s.

And like the first-time home buyer, you probably need your tax shelter benefits "up front," if for no other reason than to help you make your mortgage payments.

Another phenomenon of the past few years is the growth in second mortgages and refinancing to capitalize on the built-up equity in home values. If you are in this category, you also need to know about IRS's new computational rules for determining increased withholding allowances.

Note: *By now you should be capable of using the Form W-4 Worksheet and computing all the withholding allowances to which you are legally entitled. You should also be capable of adjusting your withholding allowances so that you only claim the number of allowances you really need without becoming indebted to the IRS. If you're not able to perform both of those functions, you should go back and reread Chapters 2 and 3. The methods taught there are essential for your understanding of this chapter.*

THE "NEW" COMPUTATIONAL METHOD

You already know that mortgage interest and real estate tax payments are deductible on your tax return, and that both of these items can be considered for purposes of computing your additional withholding allowances. You learned in Chapter 2 that when you use the Form W-4 Worksheet, you compute your withholding allowance items based on what you reasonably expect to be able to deduct on your tax return for that year (the IRS refers to it as the "estimation year"). You also learned that in no event could you deduct an amount that exceeded the amount you deducted the previous year unless the increase was "a determinable additional amount" that is "demonstrably attributable to identifiable events" if it relates to a "binding obligation" that is "verifiable."

In this chapter you will learn the one variation to that rule. According to IRS regulation 31.3402(m)-1(d), if:

- You pay or accrue amounts "demonstrably attributable to identifiable events" (as defined in Chapter 2) that are:
  (a) interest that is attributable to ownership of real property and deductible under the Code, or
  (b) state, local or foreign real property taxes, or
  (c) a proportionate share of the interest or taxes paid by a tenant-stockholder to a cooperative housing corporation, and
- You are obligated to pay or accrue such amounts for at least two years after your estimation year then you may compute the portion of your estimated itemized deductions attributable to such amounts on your W-4 Worksheet using the "new" computational method. (Unlike other methods, this one has no name, so we will call it the *real-property computational method*.)

This method can be used only in the year in which the transaction occurs. And, IRS regulations are broad enough to allow you to use the method not only when buying real property for the first time, but also for real property bought when "trading up;" for second mortgages; and for refinancing arrangements. It will help you considerably in matching your withholding to your tax liability if your real estate transaction occurs in the middle of the year instead of at the beginning.

Since it can be used only in the year of the real property transaction, it is not useful for subsequent years, and the IRS requires that you recompute your withholding allowances at the end of the estimation year.

> *The real-property computational method is another averaging technique. For the remainder of the year it enables you to take advantage of your increased mortgage interest and real estate tax payments* **as if** *you had incurred the new expenses* **for the entire year.**

The value of the method to you is that it approximates your withholding more closely to your true end-of-the-year tax liability. The method involves these few quick steps:

STEP 1

Compute the mortgage interest payments and real estate taxes for which you are obligated from the date you first pay or accrue such amounts to the end of the estimation year (the year in which you are making the estimate).

STEP 2

Multiply amount in Step 1 by 12.

STEP 3

Divide the Step 2 amount by the number of months from the first month in which you pay or accrue such amounts through the last month in the estimation year. (Note: The number of months computed here may differ from the number of months your taxes may actually be withheld under this method, due to the delay between the date of the transaction and the date your new W-4 certificate takes effect. Unfortunately, the IRS makes no provision in its formula for this delay.)

STEP 4

Add to this amount the other expense items of your itemized (Schedule A) deductions, such as medical expenses, state and local taxes, other interest, etc.

STEP 5

Add to the above amount the total of all other estimated deductions, such as alimony payments, IRAs, and deduction for married couple when both work.

Total and enter on Line D-1 of W-4 Worksheet.

Example 1

Ed is single and earns $36,000 a year. He bought a condominium residence ten years ago for $43,500 when the interest rate on a mortgage was only 8.5 percent. He's been itemizing deductions ever since and claiming a sufficient number of withholding allowances so that he's never overwithheld by more than $100. He wants to adjust his withholding in 1984 with the same objective in mind.

In September 1984 Ed sold his condominium for $83,500 and bought a single detached home for $95,000 with $15,000 down. He decided to take the remainder of his gain from the sale of the condominium and invest it in the stock market. (Note: Ed will *not* have to pay tax on the $40,000 gain on the sale of his condominium this year because the purchase price of his new home is at least as much as the adjusted sale price of the old home, and he meets all the requirements for postponing his gain.) He is financing his new home with an $80,000 mortgage at 12.5 percent with principal and interest payments of $853.81 per month for thirty years beginning September 17, 1984.

Prior to buying his new home, this is what Ed's withholding and tax profile looked like:

Monthly income	$ 3,000	× 12 =	$ 36,000
Monthly withholding	$ 544.60		(6 allowances)
Mortgage interest on condo for entire year			$ 3,223
Real estate taxes on condo for entire year			$ 777
Other itemized deductions			$ 2,300
Estimated tax liability with condo for entire year			$ 6,453

Ed went to settlement on his new house on September 17 and sold his condo the same day. His mortgage payments for principal and interest increased by $531.26 per month and his annual real estate taxes went from $777 to $1,118.

Ed analyzed the interest amortization table his mortgage company gave him and computed his withholding allowances as follows:

Mortgage interest on condo from Jan. 1
thru Sept. 17 .... $ 2,295.84
Real estate taxes on condo from Jan. 1 thru Sept. 17 .... 553.48
Mortgage interest on new home from Sept. 17
thru Dec. 31 .... 2,881.99
Real estate taxes on new home from Sept. 17
thru Dec. 31 .... 321.62
Loan origination fee deductible as interest (1%) 800.00
    Total deductions related to real estate .... $ 6,852.93
    Add other itemized deductions .... + 2,300.00
Total Schedule A—Itemized Deductions .... $ 9,152.93

Ed prepared the following W-4 Worksheet showing the above:

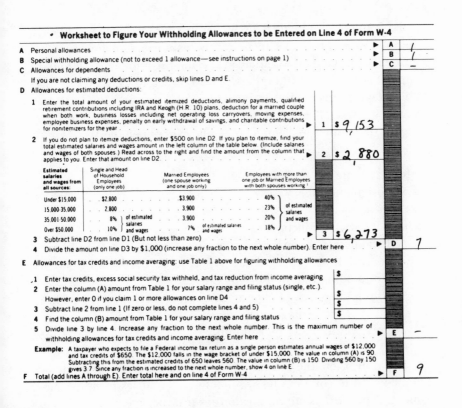

Notice that Ed increased his withholding allowances from six to nine. His withholding will now decrease from $544.60 to $461.40 per month, a monthly "savings" of $83.20. Since Ed could not submit his new W-4 Certificate to his employer until after September 17, Ed's reduced withholding will only be effective for the paychecks he receives starting in October.

Without using the real-property computational method, Ed's withholding profile would look like this:

9 months' withholding of $544.60	=	$	4,901.40
+ 3 months' withholding of $461.40	=	+	1,384.20
Total withholding	=	$	6,285.60
Tax liability	=	−	5,509.10
Overwithholding	=	$+	776.50

Ed is still overwithheld $776.50 because his increase in withholding allowances from six to nine was insufficient. In order to be properly withheld Ed would need to claim the number of withholding allowances he would otherwise be entitled to were he carrying these deductions for the entire year.

For instance, if Ed were to buy this house on Jan. 1, 1984, he would be entitled to claim *fourteen* allowances per the W-4 Worksheet using the following figures:

Mortgage interest on $80,000 at 12.5%	$ 10,000
Loan origination fee	+ 800
Real estate taxes	+ 1,118
Other itemized deductions	+ 2,300
Total itemized deductions	$ 14,218
Tax liability	$ 4,006.32
Withholding required per month	$ 333.86
Withholding per 14 allowances	$ 330.38
(percentage method)	
Underwithholding (per month)	$ 3.48

Logically, then, the correct way to handle this situation would be to allow Ed to compute his withholding allowances from the moment of the real estate transactions as if he were entitled to claim

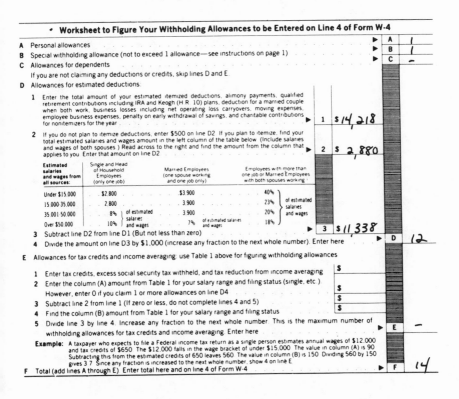

* **Worksheet to Figure Your Withholding Allowances to be Entered on Line 4 of Form W-4**

A Personal allowances .... ▶ A |

B Special withholding allowance (not to exceed 1 allowance—see instructions on page 1) .... ▶ B |

C Allowances for dependents .... ▶ C —

If you are not claiming any deductions or credits, skip lines D and E.

D Allowances for estimated deductions:

   1 Enter the total amount of your estimated itemized deductions, alimony payments, qualified retirement contributions including IRA and Keogh (H.R. 10) plans, deduction for a married couple when both work, business losses including net operating loss carryovers, moving expenses, employee business expenses, penalty on early withdrawal of savings, and charitable contributions for nonitemizers for the year .... ▶ 1 $14,218

   2 If you do not plan to itemize deductions, enter $500 on line D2. If you plan to itemize, find your total estimated salaries and wages amount in the left column of the table below. (Include salaries and wages of both spouses.) Read across to the right and find the amount from the column that applies to you. Enter that amount on line D2 .... ▶ 2 $2,880

Estimated salaries and wages from all sources:	Single and Head of Household Employees (only one job)	Married Employees (one spouse working and one job only)	Employees with more than one job or Married Employees with both spouses working
Under $15,000	$2,800	$3,900	40%
15,000-35,000	2,800	3,900	23% of estimated salaries and wages
35,001-50,000	8% of estimated salaries and wages	3,900	20%
Over $50,000	10% of estimated salaries and wages	7% of estimated salaries and wages	18%

   3 Subtract line D2 from line D1 (But not less than zero) .... ▶ 3 $11,338

   4 Divide the amount on line D3 by $1,000 (increase any fraction to the next whole number). Enter here .... ▶ D 12

E Allowances for tax credits and income averaging: use Table 1 above for figuring withholding allowances

   1 Enter tax credits, excess social security tax withheld, and tax reduction from income averaging $____

   2 Enter the column (A) amount from Table 1 for your salary range and filing status (single, etc.). However, enter 0 if you claim 1 or more allowances on line D4 $____

   3 Subtract line 2 from line 1 (If zero or less, do not complete lines 4 and 5) $____

   4 Find the column (B) amount from Table 1 for your salary range and filing status $____

   5 Divide line 3 by line 4. Increase any fraction to the next whole number. This is the maximum number of withholding allowances for tax credits and income averaging. Enter here .... ▶ E —

   Example: A taxpayer who expects to file a Federal income tax return as a single person estimates annual wages of $12,000 and tax credits of $650. The $12,000 falls in the wage bracket of under $15,000. The value in column (A) is 90. Subtracting this from the estimated credits of 650 leaves 560. The value in column (B) is 150. Dividing 560 by 150 gives 3.7. Since any fraction is increased to the next whole number, show 4 on line E.

F Total (add lines A through E). Enter total here and on line 4 of Form W-4 .... ▶ F 14

the fourteen allowances over the next twelve months, instead of just the remaining months in the calendar year.

This inequity continued to exist until February 1983, when the IRS issued new regulations allowing use of the real-property computational method. Using the "new" method, Ed would figure his withholding allowances as follows:

STEP 1

Compute the new mortgage interest payments and real estate taxes and other real estate fees for which you are obligated, from the date you first pay or accrue them to the end of the estimation year ($2,881.99 + $321.62 + $800) .... $ 4,003.61

STEP 2

Multiply amount in Step 1 by 12 .... × ____12____

Equals 48,043.32

STEP 3

Divide Step 2 amount by the number of months,
from the first month in which you pay or accrue such
amounts through the last month in the estimation year

.... ÷ ____4____

Equals $12,010.83

STEP 4

Add to the amount in Step 3 the other expense items
for your total itemized deductions when using the W-4
Worksheet:

Previous mortgage and real estate deductions ... + $ 2,849.32

All other Schedule A itemized deductions .... + $ 2,300.00

Total itemized Schedule A deductions $17,160.15

STEP 5

Add above amount to the total of all other estimated
deductions such as alimony payments, IRAs, deduction
for married couple when both work, etc. (See items
listed on Line D-1 of W-4 Worksheet.) .... + ____0____

Total and enter on Line D-1 of W-4 Worksheet ... $ __17,160__

Using the real-property computational method, Ed's withholding
and tax profile now looks like this:

9 months' withholding of $ 544.60	=	$ 4,901.40	(6 allwns.)
3 months' withholding of $ 267.87	=	+ 803.61	(17 allwns.)
Total withholding	=	$ 5,705.01	
Tax liability	=	$ 5,509.10	
Overwithholding	=	$ 195.91	

By using the real-property computational method, Ed has reduced his overwithholding from $776.50 using the standard
method to $195.91, a further decrease in withholding of $580.59.

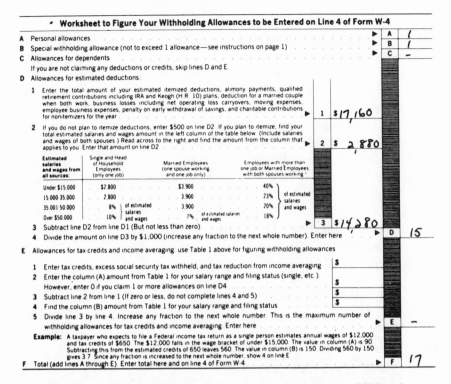

• Worksheet to Figure Your Withholding Allowances to be Entered on Line 4 of Form W-4

A Personal allowances .... ▶ | A | *1*
B Special withholding allowance (not to exceed 1 allowance—see instructions on page 1) .... ▶ | B | *1*
C Allowances for dependents .... ▶ | C | *—*
  If you are not claiming any deductions or credits, skip lines D and E.
D Allowances for estimated deductions:

  1 Enter the total amount of your estimated itemized deductions, alimony payments, qualified retirement contributions including IRA and Keogh (H.R. 10) plans, deduction for a married couple when both work, business losses including net operating loss carryovers, moving expenses, employee business expenses, penalty on early withdrawal of savings, and charitable contributions for nonitemizers for the year .... ▶ | 1 | $ *17,160*

  2 If you do not plan to itemize deductions, enter $500 on line D2. If you plan to itemize, find your total estimated salaries and wages amount in the left column of the table below. (Include salaries and wages of both spouses.) Read across to the right and find the amount from the column that applies to you. Enter that amount on line D2 .... ▶ | 2 | $ *2,880*

Estimated salaries and wages from all sources:	Single and Head of Household Employees (only one job)	Married Employees (one spouse working and one job only)	Employees with more than one job or Married Employees with both spouses working
Under $15,000	$2,800	$3,900	40% ⎫
15,000-35,000	2,800	3,900	23% ⎬ of estimated salaries
35,001-50,000	8% ⎫ of estimated salaries and wages	3,900	20% ⎭ and wages
Over $50,000	10% ⎭	7% of estimated salaries and wages	18%

  3 Subtract line D2 from line D1 (But not less than zero) .... ▶ | 3 | $ *14,280*
  4 Divide the amount on line D3 by $1,000 (increase any fraction to the next whole number). Enter here ▶ | D | *15*

E Allowances for tax credits and income averaging: use Table 1 above for figuring withholding allowances

  1 Enter tax credits, excess social security tax withheld, and tax reduction from income averaging | $
  2 Enter the column (A) amount from Table 1 for your salary range and filing status (single, etc.). However, enter 0 if you claim 1 or more allowances on line D4 | $
  3 Subtract line 2 from line 1 (If zero or less, do not complete lines 4 and 5) | $
  4 Find the column (B) amount from Table 1 for your salary range and filing status | $
  5 Divide line 3 by line 4. Increase any fraction to the next whole number. This is the maximum number of withholding allowances for tax credits and income averaging. Enter here .... ▶ | E | *—*

  Example: A taxpayer who expects to file a Federal income tax return as a single person estimates annual wages of $12,000 and tax credits of $650. The $12,000 falls in the wage bracket of under $15,000. The value in column (A) is 90. Subtracting this from the estimated credits of 650 leaves 560. The value in column (B) is 150. Dividing 560 by 150 gives 3.7. Since any fraction is increased to the next whole number, show 4 on line E.

F Total (add lines A through E). Enter total here and on line 4 of Form W-4 .... ▶ | F | *17*

This means that Ed is able to increase his paycheck by an additional $193.53 a month for the months of October, November, and December. If Ed had been able to submit his new W-4 to his employer in time to reduce his withholding in his September check, he would have no overwithholding.

Caution: If there are joint incomes or if you are working two jobs, this method may result in underwithholding. You must use the worksheet in Chapter 3 to adjust your allowances after you've computed your total itemized deductions using the real-property computational method.

Example 2

Anita and Steve, who have a combined income of $42,000 a year, bought their first home on July 1, 1984. They have no dependents and have never itemized their deductions before.

Because Anita and Steve both work, they have each been claiming zero allowances, plus Steve has had an additional $29 a month withheld to compensate for being underwithheld.

Their home cost $100,000 and, with $10,000 down, they are carrying a $90,000 mortgage at 12 percent interest, with principal and interest payments of $925.26 a month. For the period July 1 through December 31, they will have $5,396 in interest deductions and a $600 deduction for real estate taxes. Their total itemized deductions for 1984 will be $9,300 (including $3,304 for other items).

Using the Form W-4 Worksheet, Steve figures that he will be able to increase his withholding allowances from zero plus $29 extra to four. Anita will continue claiming zero allowances.

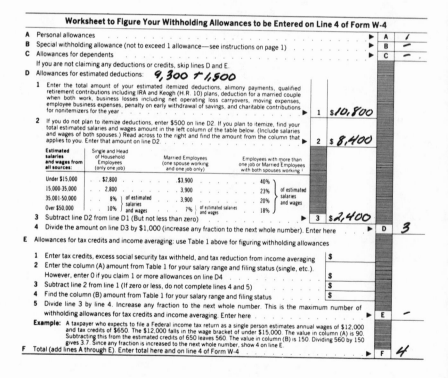

Worksheet to Figure Your Withholding Allowances to be Entered on Line 4 of Form W-4

A Personal allowances ▶ **A** _1_

B Special withholding allowance (not to exceed 1 allowance—see instructions on page 1) ▶ **B** _—_

C Allowances for dependents ▶ **C** _—_

If you are not claiming any deductions or credits, skip lines D and E.

D Allowances for estimated deductions: *9,300 + 1,500*

1 Enter the total amount of your estimated itemized deductions, alimony payments, qualified retirement contributions including IRA and Keogh (H.R. 10) plans, deduction for a married couple when both work, business losses including net operating loss carryovers, moving expenses, employee business expenses, penalty on early withdrawal of savings, and charitable contributions for nonitemizers for the year ▶ **1** $*10,800*

2 If you do not plan to itemize deductions, enter $500 on line D2. If you plan to itemize, find your total estimated salaries and wages amount in the left column of the table below. (Include salaries and wages of both spouses.) Read across to the right and find the amount from the column that applies to you. Enter that amount on line D2. ▶ **2** $*8,400*

Estimated salaries and wages from all sources:	Single and Head of Household Employees (only one job)	Married Employees (one spouse working and one job only)	Employees with more than one job or Married Employees with both spouses working [1]
Under $15,000	. . $2,800	. . . . $3,900	. . . . 40%
15,000-35,000	. . 2,800	 3,900	. . . . 23%	of estimated salaries and wages
35,001-50,000	8% } of estimated salaries and wages	 3,900	. . . . 20%
Over $50,000	10% }	. . . 7% { of estimated salaries and wages	. . . . 18%

3 Subtract line D2 from line D1 (But not less than zero) ▶ **3** $*2,400*

4 Divide the amount on line D3 by $1,000 (increase any fraction to the next whole number). Enter here ▶ **D** _3_

E Allowances for tax credits and income averaging: use Table 1 above for figuring withholding allowances

1 Enter tax credits, excess social security tax withheld, and tax reduction from income averaging $

2 Enter the column (A) amount from Table 1 for your salary range and filing status (single, etc.). However, enter 0 if you claim 1 or more allowances on line D4 $

3 Subtract line 2 from line 1 (If zero or less, do not complete lines 4 and 5) $

4 Find the column (B) amount from Table 1 for your salary range and filing status $

5 Divide line 3 by line 4. Increase any fraction to the next whole number. This is the maximum number of withholding allowances for tax credits and income averaging. Enter here ▶ **E** _—_

Example: A taxpayer who expects to file a Federal income tax return as a single person estimates annual wages of $12,000 and tax credits of $650. The $12,000 falls in the wage bracket of under $15,000. The value in column (A) is 90. Subtracting this from the estimated credits of 650 leaves 560. The value in column (B) is 150. Dividing 560 by 150 gives 3.7. Since any fraction is increased to the next whole number, show 4 on line E.

F Total (add lines A through E). Enter total here and on line 4 of Form W-4 ▶ **F** _4_

Without using the real-property computational method, their withholding profile looks like this:

Income per Month	Withholding		Total
Steve $ 1,500	− 6 months at $ 220	= $	1,320.00
(4 allowances)	− 6 months at $134.30	= +	805.80
Anita $ 2,000	− 12 months at $302.10	= +	3,625.20
	Total tax withheld	= $	5,751.00
	Tax liability	= −	5,432.00
	Overwithheld	= $	319.00

Using the real-property computational method, their withholding looks like this:

STEP 1

Compute the mortgage interest payments and real estate taxes for which you are obligated, from the date you first pay or accrue such amounts to the end of the estimation year ($5,396 + $600) . . . . $ ___5,996

STEP 2

Multiply amount in Step 1 by 12 . . . . × ___12

Equals . . . . $ ___71,952

STEP 3

Divide Step 2 amount by the number of months from the first month in which you pay or accrue such amounts through the last month in the estimation year . . . . ÷ ___6

Equals . . . . $ 11,992

STEP 4

Add to the amount in Step 3 the other expense items for your total itemized deductions when using the W-4 Worksheet:

Previous mortgage and real estate deductions . . . . + ___0

All other Schedule A itemized deductions . . . . + 3,304.00

Total Schedule A itemized deductions . . . . $ 15,296.00

STEP 5

Add above amount to the total of all other estimated
deductions, such as alimony payments, IRAs, deduction
for married couple when both work, etc. (See items
listed on Line D-1 of W-4 Worksheet.) . . . . +   1,800

Total and enter on Line D-1 of W-4 Worksheet . . . $ 17,096

Notice that in this case the real-property computational method
actually doubled Steve's deduction for his mortgage interest payments and real estate taxes. Even though this is not the exact
amount of Steve's payment, and certainly *not* the amount he can
deduct on his tax return, it is the amount he can use for purposes of
computing his number of withholding allowances.

Steve fills out a new W-4 Worksheet using the above figures and
computes that he is now allowed to claim *ten* allowances.

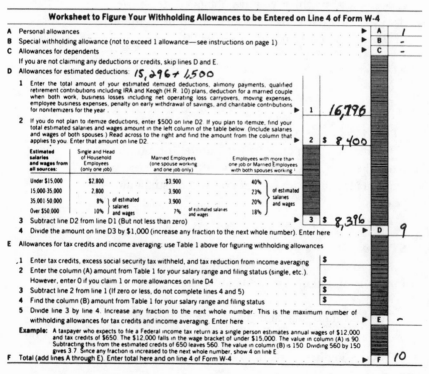

Worksheet to Figure Your Withholding Allowances to be Entered on Line 4 of Form W-4

A Personal allowances ▶ **A** *1*

B Special withholding allowance (not to exceed 1 allowance—see instructions on page 1) ▶ **B** *-*

C Allowances for dependents ▶ **C** *-*

  If you are not claiming any deductions or credits, skip lines D and E.

D Allowances for estimated deductions: *15,296 + 1,500*

  1 Enter the total amount of your estimated itemized deductions, alimony payments, qualified retirement contributions including IRA and Keogh (H.R. 10) plans, deduction for a married couple when both work, business losses including net operating loss carryovers, moving expenses, employee business expenses, penalty on early withdrawal of savings, and charitable contributions for nonitemizers for the year ▶ **1** *16,796*

  2 If you do not plan to itemize deductions, enter $500 on line D2. If you plan to itemize, find your total estimated salaries and wages amount in the left column of the table below. (Include salaries and wages of both spouses.) Read across to the right and find the amount from the column that applies to you. Enter that amount on line D2. ▶ **2** $ *8,400*

Estimated salaries and wages from all sources:	Single and Head of Household Employees (only one job)	Married Employees (one spouse working and one job only)	Employees with more than one job or Married Employees with both spouses working
Under $15,000	$2,800	$3,900	40%
15,000-35,000	2,800	3,900	23% } of estimated
35,001-50,000	8% } of estimated	3,900	20% } salaries and wages
Over $50,000	10% } salaries and wages	7% } of estimated salaries and wages	18% }

  3 Subtract line D2 from line D1 (But not less than zero) ▶ **3** $ *8,396*

  4 Divide the amount on line D3 by $1,000 (increase any fraction to the next whole number). Enter here ▶ **D** *9*

E Allowances for tax credits and income averaging: use Table 1 above for figuring withholding allowances

  1 Enter tax credits, excess social security tax withheld, and tax reduction from income averaging $

  2 Enter the column (A) amount from Table 1 for your salary range and filing status (single, etc.). However, enter 0 if you claim 1 or more allowances on line D4 $

  3 Subtract line 2 from line 1 (If zero or less, do not complete lines 4 and 5) $

  4 Find the column (B) amount from Table 1 for your salary range and filing status $

  5 Divide line 3 by line 4. Increase any fraction to the next whole number. This is the maximum number of withholding allowances for tax credits and income averaging. Enter here ▶ **E** *-*

  Example: A taxpayer who expects to file a Federal income tax return as a single person estimates annual wages of $12,000 and tax credits of $650. The $12,000 falls in the wage bracket of under $15,000. The value in column (A) is 90. Subtracting this from the estimated credits of 650 leaves 560. The value in column (B) is 150. Dividing 560 by 150 gives 3.7. Since any fraction is increased to the next whole number, show 4 on line E.

F Total (add lines A through E). Enter total here and on line 4 of Form W-4 ▶ **F** *10*

Steve and Anita's withholding profile now looks like this:

Income per Month	Withholding		Total
Steve $ 1,500	− 6 months at $ 220	= $	1,320.00
(10 allowances)	− 6 months at $ 56	= +	336.00
Anita $ 2,000	− 12 months at $302.10	= +	3,625.20
	Total tax withheld	= $	5,281.20
	Tax liability	= −	5,432.00
	Underwithheld	= $	150.80

If you recall from Chapter 3, Steve must decide if he wants to be underwithheld $150.80 or if he would like his withholding to be a little closer to his actual tax liability. To figure the number of allowances that would be closer to his actual taxes, Steve would use the worksheet in Chapter 3.

This method resulted in Steve being underwithheld because of the joint income factor. But notice that Steve's withholding is sufficient not to require him to make estimated tax payments, and his underwithholding will not even cause him to be penalized since more than 80 percent of his actual tax liability is covered by withholding (actually 95 percent in Steve's case).

The real-property computational method is very quick and easy to compute. Before you use the worksheet at the end of the chapter, you need to know the following:

- The IRS will *not* allow you to use this method if you are using the cumulative-wages method (as explained in Chapter 6). Even though the cumulative-wages method is an averaging technique for wages and the real-property computational method is an averaging technique for certain itemized deductions, the IRS believes that using the two methods together will cause much confusion and lead to underwithholding.
- Examine your settlement sheet to see if you have paid other settlement expenses that could be considered to be interest such as "loan origination fees" or "points." But be very careful, the IRS has a lot of rules on what "points" are deductible and what aren't. See the box on page 83 for guidance. If you're still

not clear, check with your local IRS office or your tax adviser.

- You *must remember* to recompute your withholding allowances using the standard method before the beginning of the new year. Your new W-4 Certificate should be submitted by December 1.

- If you end up claiming more than fourteen allowances and you get a letter of inquiry from the IRS, explain to them what transactional event relating to real property has just occurred (e.g., purchase of new home), and specify that you are computing your allowances under IRS Regulation 31.3402(m)-1(d). But don't be afraid of an IRS inquiry letter; it's normal procedure with their crackdown on abusive W-4 Certificates.

- If you have two jobs or you and your spouse are both employed, you *must* follow up the real-property computational method with the worksheet in Chapter 3 for adjusting your allowances.

YOUR WORKSHEET FOR USING THE REAL-PROPERTY COMPUTATIONAL METHOD

Before using this worksheet you need the following information:

- Your mortgage interest and real estate tax payments paid at settlement, plus the amounts of any "points" or "loan origination fees" clearly deductible on your tax return as interest.
- Your mortgage interest and real estate tax payments due after settlement through the end of the year.
- The amount you estimate for all your other itemized deductions, including mortgage interest and real estate tax payments for real property previously owned.

Note: The worksheet on the following page is a slightly lengthier version than the one used in the examples. The methodology is exactly the same, but all the additions are made on the worksheet instead of off to the side. This will help you keep track of all your deductions and minimize the possibility of overlooking anything.

Excerpt From IRS Publication 17

"Points" paid by a borrower. The term "points" is sometimes used to describe certain charges paid by a borrower. They are also called loan origination fees, maximum loan charges, or premium charges. If the payment of any of these charges is **only** for the use of money, it is interest.

These points are interest paid in advance and, generally, you may not deduct the full amount for points in the year paid. The prepaid interest paid as points must be spread over the life of the mortgage, and is considered as paid and is deductible over that period.

Exception. You may deduct the amount you pay as points in the year of payment if the loan is used to buy or improve your principal home and is secured by that home.

This exception will only apply if—

1) The payment of points is an established business practice in the area where the loan was made, and
2) The points paid did not exceed the number of points generally charged in this area.

If you paid more points than generally paid in this area, your deduction is limited to the points generally charged. Any additional amount of points you paid is interest paid in advance.

Points charged for specific services by the lender for the borrower's account are not interest. Examples of fees for services not considered interest are the lender's appraisal fee, preparation costs for the mortgage note or deed of trust, settlement fees, and notary fees. Points charged for services for getting a Veterans Administration loan are not interest. See *Example 2.*

Expenses you pay in connection with a mortgage as commissions, abstract fees, and recording fees, are capital expenses. You may not deduct these expenses either as interest or as current business expenses.

Example 1. Don Smith borrowed $48,000 to buy his $60,000 home. He paid the lender, in addition to interest at 13%, a loan processing fee of $1,440 (three points). None of the fee was for specific services. The charging of points was an established business practice in the area and the number of points was not more than that generally charged in the area. The $1,440 loan processing fee (points) is interest. Don may deduct it in the year of payment.

Example 2. Jan Green got a loan from a bank to buy her home. The loan was insured by the Veterans Administration. Jan paid the bank a loan origination fee. The fee was 1% of the amount of the loan. It was charged in addition to the maximum rate of interest permitted. The 1% loan origination fee (one point) is not interest. Jan may not deduct it.

"Points" paid by a seller. The term "points" also is used to describe loan placement fees that the seller may have to pay to the lender to arrange financing for the buyer. The seller may *not* deduct these amounts as interest. But these charges are a selling expense that reduce the amount realized.

YOUR WORKSHEET FOR USING THE REAL PROPERTY COMPUTATIONAL METHOD

STEP 1

Add the mortgage interest payments .... $ _____

and the real estate taxes .... + _____

for which you are obligated, from the date you first
pay or accrue such amounts to the end of the
estimation year,

Equals .... _____

STEP 2

Multiply amount in Step 1 by 12 .... × ____12____

Equals .... _____

STEP 3

Divide Step 2 amount by the number of months from
the first month in which you pay or accrue such
amounts through the last month in the estimation
year .... ÷ _____

Equals .... _____

STEP 4

Add to the Step 3 amount the following itemized (Schedule A)
deductions:

- Medical expenses .... + _____
- Taxes (including taxes on previous residence) ... + _____
- Interest expenses (including previous
  mortgage interest) .... + _____
- Contributions .... + _____
- Casualty and theft losses .... + _____
- Miscellaneous deductions .... + _____
- Total (Step 3 + above items) itemized deductions
  (without subtracting zero bracket
  amount on Schedule A) .... _____

STEP 5

Add the total in Step 4 to the following items:

- Alimony payments .... + _____
- Moving expenses (see IRS Form 3903) .... + _____
- Deduction for married couple when both
  work (Schedule W − 10% of lower income) .... + _____
- Losses from Schedules C, D, E, F, and Form 4797 + _____
- Net operating loss carry-over from previous year + _____
- Penalty or early withdrawal of savings .... + _____
- Retirement contributions like Keogh, IRA, & SEP + _____
- Employee business expenses .... + _____
  Total, and enter on Line D-1 of W-4
  Worksheet on page 30 .... _____

CHAPTER FIVE

The Part-Year Employment Method

This chapter applies only to those who work part of the year only.

Question: I have an unusual situation. I don't work a full year, but when I'm working, I'm usually working full-time. I always earn enough money to file a tax return, and even have a tax liability, so I can't file a W-4 Exemption from Withholding. What happens is that I usually get a large refund. I was told that the tax is withheld at the rate that would apply if I was earning the same money all year. I don't understand this, but is there anything I can do to ease the tax bite from each paycheck?

Answer: Yes. The IRS has regulations to fit circumstances such as yours. What is happening to you is that your tax withholding is based on the presumption that you will be in the same income tax bracket throughout the year. The tax tables are set up for that because that is the norm. But by not earning the same income throughout the year you actually end up in a lower tax bracket.

If you work only part of the year, the IRS provides a method for withholding lesser amounts of income tax, by averaging in weeks of employment with the weeks of unemployment to compute your withholding.

For example, suppose you are single, earn $300 a week, and claim only one allowance. Your income tax withholding would be

$41.00, or 13.67 percent of your income, each payday. If you earned this same salary fifty-two weeks a year, your taxable income (assuming no itemized deductions, adjustments, or tax credits) would be $14,560 (52 × $300 = $15,600 − $1,040 exemption) for a tax liability of $1,872.60 (12.0 percent of your gross income). With a total tax withheld of $2,132.00, you would receive a refund of $259.40.

However, if you only work six months, you will have earned $7,800 and your withheld tax will be $1,066.00 (13.67 percent). But when you file your tax return and report a gross income of $7,800, you discover that your actual tax liability is only $556.50 (7.1 percent of your gross income), producing a refund of $509.50. As you can see, the income actually earned for the part year produced a tax liability of 7.1 percent of your gross income, whereas the tax was withheld at a rate of 13.67 percent of your gross income, resulting in a much larger refund than necessary, or even of what was required to be withheld by the government.

The IRS provides a method for withholding lesser amounts of income taxes in situations like this, the *part-year employment method*. Under this method your income is computed each payday by averaging your weeks of employment with your weeks of unemployment when there was no income. For example, if you don't work for thirteen weeks and then become employed, your first weekly paycheck is averaged with the thirteen weeks you weren't working to produce an average weekly income for the combined period. The income tax withholding for the first payroll period is then based on the average weekly income for that period.

For payroll periods after the first week, each succeeding week is averaged with the previous weeks of employment plus the weeks of unemployment. This produces a gradually increasing rate of income tax withholding until the amount withheld comes close to matching the amount that would have been withheld had the method not been used. The part-year employment method is calculated to save you tax money "up front." The more income you have, obviously, the greater your savings will be. The end result is a bigger paycheck and less money being "saved" for you by the IRS. This could be especially important for you if you only work part of the year; you may need the extra money now, this year, rather than next year after you file your tax return.

If you want your income tax withholding to be computed using this method, you must make your request to your employer in writing, under penalties of perjury, specifying the following information as true:

- The last day you were employed during the current calendar year with any prior employer.
- That you reasonably anticipate that you do not expect to be employed more than 245 days of continuous employment, *counting all employers*. (See the definition of continuous employment below.)
- That you use the calendar year accounting period (from January 1 through December 31) and not a fiscal year period (normally, only businesses use a fiscal year accounting period).

But don't be surprised if your employer balks. It is really quite a complicated procedure, and not too many employers understand how to compute it, even if they read the regulations themselves; and none of the IRS publications give examples of the computations. So if you fall into a part-year employment situation, you should read and study the following example, which will help you understand how this method may help you "save" tax dollars. First you need to understand the IRS phrase *term of continuous employment*. A term of continuous employment with a given employer:

- Starts on the first day you earn compensation from your employer.
- May be a single term, or two or more consecutive terms with the same employer.
- Could include a temporary layoff of less than thirty days; but it is ended if your employment relationship is terminated (i.e., you were fired or quit), even if you reestablish an employment relationship within thirty days.
- Includes not only the days you are actually working but also the days you are sick, on vacation, or not working due to holidays or regular days off. For example, if you regularly work only two days a week, your term of continuous employment includes the entire week.

The part-year employment method is a complicated six-step process, but by studying the following example carefully, you will be able to see how important it may be to you.

Example

Laurie was a self-employed, part-time consultant in 1983, but in 1984 landed a solid six-month employment contract with one of her clients, Washington Management Services (WMS), who offered to pay her $1,000 a week for twenty-six weeks. Her contract began on April 22 and terminated on October 18. She was unemployed and had no consulting work from January 1 through April 21 (111 days). She is single and claimed two withholding allowances on her W-4 Certificate. Realizing that her income tax withholding would occur at the same percentage rate as for someone making $52,000 a year ($264.60 per week to be precise), she made a written request to her employer for her withholding to be computed using the part-year employment method. Her request is illustrated on page 90. In Laurie's case, there is only one term of continuous employment during the year.

Laurie's personnel manager winced when he received the memo. He checked the instructions in the latest edition of IRS Publication 15 (also known as Circular E, "Employers Tax Guide") and computed her withholding using the six-step approach. Review Laurie's worksheet on page 91, studying the six-step approach for each week, paying close attention to the results specified here.

FIRST WEEK. As you can clearly see, Laurie has just increased her first paycheck by $264.60, the amount that would have been withheld had she not requested that her employer use the part-year employment method.

Note that the number "15" used in Step 2 is the number of payroll periods between Laurie's last employment (or the previous December 31, if later), and the first day of her current employment. This is computed by dividing the number of unemployed calendar days by the number of calendar days in this payroll period; example: 111 ÷ 7 = 15.85, but dropping the fraction, per IRS rules, equals "15."

TO: Personnel Manager, Washington Management Services

FROM: Laurie

RE: Withholding of Income Taxes Under the Part-Year
         Employment Method

This request is made under IRS Regulation 31.3402(h) (4)-1(c)(5). I am requesting that my income tax be withheld using the part-year employment method, and the following information is being furnished to you as required by the above cited IRS regulation:

(a) There is no last day of employment with any employer prior to this current term of continuous employment during this calendar year,

(b) I reasonably anticipate that I will not be employed for more than 245 days in all terms of continuous employment during this calendar year,

(c) I use the calendar-year accounting period.

I hereby certify, under penalties of perjury, that the information supplied herein is true and correct.

Sincerely,

Laurie

SECOND WEEK. Notice that Laurie has again saved money from going to the IRS needlessly. The amount "saved" is $157.50 ($264.60 that would have been withheld, less $107.10, the amount actually withheld). So far, for the first two weeks on the job, she has "saved" $422.10 ($264.60 from the first week plus $157.50 for this week) from going to the IRS.

THIRD WEEK. This time Laurie has saved $130.50 ($264.60 less $134.10). So far Laurie has "saved" a total of $552.60, just three weeks on the job.

OPTIONAL WORKSHEET: PART-YEAR EMPLOYMENT METHOD—LAURIE: 1984

PAYROLL PERIOD	WEEK 1 (April 22)	WEEK 2 (April 29)	WEEK 3 (May 6)	WEEK 4 (May 13)
STEP 1: Enter the wages to be paid you for this payroll period.....	$1,000.00	$1,000.00	$1,000.00	$1,000.00
Add the wages already paid you in this current term of employment..............	+ -0-	+1,000.00*	+2,000.00*	+3,000.00*
Equals.................	= 1,000.00	= 2,000.00	= 3,000.00	= 4,000.00
STEP 2: Enter the number of payroll periods used in Step 1....... Add the number of payroll periods between your last employment (or the previous Dec. 31, whichever is later) and the first day of your current employment........	1	2**	3**	4**
	+15	+15	+15	+15
Equals........	= 16	= 17	= 18	= 19
STEP 3: Divide the amount from Step 1 by the total number of payroll periods from Step 2 .... ÷				
Equals..........	= $62.50	= $117.65	$166.66	$210.53
STEP 4: Find the tax in the tax withholding tables on the Step 3 amount using the table for: (write in the correct answer) > marital status ___ > payroll status ___ > number of allowances on W-4 ___	-0-	6.30	13.40	20.90
STEP 5: Multiply the Step 4 amount by the total number of payroll periods from Step 2	×16	×17	×18	×19
Equals..........	= -0-	= 107.10	241.20	397.10
STEP 6: Subtract from the Step 5 amount the total tax already withheld during the current term of continuous employment	- 0	- 0	- 107.10	- 241.20
The excess (if any) is the amount to withhold for the current payroll period	= 0	= 107.10	= 134.10	= 155.90

*The figure on this line will always be the total sum of Step 1 in the immediately preceding payroll period.
**The figure on this line will always increase by "1" from the number used in the immediately preceding payroll period.

FOURTH WEEK. This time Laurie has "saved" $108.70 ($264.60 less $155.90). So far Laurie has "saved" a total of $661.30 after just four weeks on the job.

You may have noticed that Laurie's income tax withholding increased each pay period. It will continue to increase as long as she works.

Note: *Immediately following is your optional worksheet for the part-year employment method. You are not required to use this worksheet because your income tax withholding is computed and withheld by your employer. All you have to do is to make your request in writing (under penalties of perjury). However, the optional worksheet is provided here for several groups of taxpayers:*

• *For those who worked part-time last year and would like to find out how much they would have "saved" had they used the part-year employment method. (For this you will need last year's withholding tables. You can only use this year's withholding tables if you compare the withholding to this year's tax tables.)*

• *For those who are working part-time this year and would like to determine how much they will "save" by using the part-year employment method.*

• *For those who work for small companies and would like to teach their employers (or their employer's payroll clerk) how to compute their withholding under the part-year employment method.*

• *For those employers reading this book who would like to acquaint their employees with the part-year employment method and need a worksheet to help them make the computations.*

INSTRUCTIONS FOR USE OF
THE OPTIONAL WORKSHEET

Make sure you use the correct withholding tables. The withholding tables for 1984 are *not* the same for 1985. Beginning on January 1, 1985, the tax tables and the tax withholding tables have been adjusted to the Consumer Price Index, or what is commonly referred to as "indexed for inflation."

If you worked part-time last year and you would like to find out how much you could have "saved" *last year* by using the part-year employment method, you will need the proper withholding table for 1984. Call your local IRS office and ask them to send you a copy of the proper wage bracket table for your marital status and payroll period. Also, it's possible that your employer may still have this information in his files.

The extra "savings" is the difference between what was actually withheld and the amount that would have been withheld under the part-year employment method. You may want to ask yourself if you could have used that "savings" last year. This is an especially important consideration if you only worked part-time, through no choice of yours, and you had financial obligations and responsibilities requiring a full-time income.

The worksheet may be helpful to you if you are working part-time in 1985 and you would like to find out what kind of "savings" to expect under the part-year employment method. You must use the 1985 withholding tables, which are in Appendix 1 at the back of this book. Make sure you use the appropriate wage bracket table for your marital status (single or married) and your payroll period (weekly, biweekly, semimonthly, or monthly).

When using the optional worksheet, your first payroll period of employment goes under Column 1, and continues until either the employment ends or you reach the last payroll period in which wages are to be paid within the calendar year.

The optional worksheet only has five weekly payroll periods, but you can expand this format to fit your entire period of employment using additional paper with blank lines marked to correspond to each step.

YOUR OPTIONAL WORKSHEET: PART-YEAR EMPLOYMENT METHOD

PAYROLL PERIOD	WEEK 1
STEP 1: Enter the wages to be paid you for this payroll period	$_____
Add the wages already paid you in this current term of employment	+_____
Equals	=_____
STEP 2: Enter the number of payroll periods used in Step 1	_____
Add the number of payroll periods between your last employment (or the previous Dec. 31, whichever is later) and the first day of your current employment ..	+_____
Equals	=_____
STEP 3: Divide the amount from Step 1 by the total number of payroll periods from Step 2 _____ ÷ _____	=$_____

STEP 4: Find the tax in the tax withholding tables on the Step 3 amount using the table for (write in the correct answer):
  > marital status _____
  > payroll status _____
  > number of allowances on W-4 _____
	_____

STEP 5: Multiply the Step 4 amount by the total number of payroll periods from Step 2	×_____
Equals	=_____
STEP 6: Subtract from the Step 5 amount the total tax already withheld during the current term of continuous employment	−_____
The excess (if any) is the amount to withhold from the current payroll period	=_____

WEEK 2	WEEK 3	WEEK 4	WEEK 5
$____	$____	$____	$____
+_____*	+_____*	+_____*	+_____*
=____	=____	=____	=____
____**	____**	____**	____
+___	+___	+___	+___
=___	=___	=___	=___
= $___	= $___	= $___	= $___
____	____	____	____
× ____	× ____	× ____	× ____
= ____	= ____	= ____	= ____
− ____	− ____	− ____	− ____
= ____	= ____	= ____	= ____

he figure on this line will always be the total sum of Step 1 in the immediately preceding payroll period.
he figure on this line will always increase by "1" from the number used in the immediately preceding payroll period.

CHAPTER 6

The Cumulative-Wages Method

This chapter applies to taxpayers whose
- *Income fluctuates greatly each pay period (such as experienced by commissioned salespeople).*
- *Income is steady, but will take, or has taken, a dramatic increase during the last half of the year.*
- *Number of withholding allowances will greatly change or has already done so.*

Question: I'm a salesman for a large company, but my commissions are erratic and fluctuate greatly due to seasonal and other cyclical influences. During my good months I may earn two or three times more than I earn during my bad months. I'm always overwithheld and would like to end this overwithholding problem. What should I do?

Answer: The IRS has a withholding method for employees whose income is not consistent from one pay period to the next. The *cumulative-wages method* is an averaging technique that eliminates most of the major fluctuations in income and withholding. It is especially valuable for commissioned salespeople and for those employees whose income has dramatically increased during the year. It can also be used for those who have a major change in their number of withholding allowances. The cumulative-wages method is allowed under IRS Regulation 31.3402(h)(3)-1.

The cumulative-wages method is computed in a similar manner to the part-year employment method. In a nutshell, the current pay period is averaged with all the previous pay periods in the calendar year to find an average income upon which a withholding amount is computed. That withholding amount is then multiplied by the number of the payroll period within the calendar year that the income is actually being paid, to arrive at a cumulative amount of withholding. (For example, if it's the ninth pay period, the multiplier will be nine.) The amount of taxes already withheld in the previous pay periods is then subtracted from the cumulative amount to find the amount to be withheld for that particular pay period.

The disadvantage of this method is that a new and separate computation must be made for each payroll period. But with employers' increasingly turning to computers for their bookkeeping chores, this computation could be performed just as easily as any other.

The advantage to you, the employee, is obvious: The net result is a continuous averaging process that more closely approximates your true tax liability for the year. Overwithholding occurs when there are dramatic and sometimes extreme variations in income during the year. This is because the withholding tables at high income levels require withholding at disproportionately higher percentages.

The cumulative-wages method will prevent many commissioned salespeople and others with dramatic increases in income from being unnecessarily overwithheld by tremendous amounts that can sometimes exceed thousands of dollars over a twelve-month period.

If you are a salaried employee whose earnings are fairly consistent each payday but you need to change the number of your withholding allowances, you should also consider using this method. (To learn how to adapt to a major increase in withholding allowances due to an increase in mortgage interest payments, see Chapter four.)

In order to use the cumulative-wages method, you must request it of your employer. This can be on any form your employer prescribes, but it must be in writing. The IRS doesn't provide a form for this, but your request should read something like the following:

"I hereby request that my income taxes be withheld under the cumulative-wages method as provided by IRS Regulation 31.3402(h)(3)-1. This request is effective until I give you a notice of revocation in writing."

The IRS says your request "shall be effective and may be acted upon" by your employer. To go off the cumulative-wages method, you need to also make that request in writing.

The cumulative-wages method is a four-step method that is not too complicated, provided your employer either understands how to use the percentage method of withholding or has his or her payroll bookkeeping system set up to accommodate it.

To understand how the cumulative-wages method may be able to help "save" you from overwithholding, you should review the examples that follow on pages 99 and 103. Example 1 is an example of an employee who has steady income, but with a dramatic increase in the last half of the year. Example 2 is an example of a commissioned salesperson who has erratic and drastic changes in income from month to month.

Before proceeding with the examples, you may want to review the section in Appendix 1 that explains how to compute income tax withholding using the percentage method. It may be helpful for you to understand how to use this method because:

- You will be better able to understand the examples as we show significant "savings" of withholdings using the cumulative-wages method.
- You will be better able to make your own computations if you want to use the optional worksheets at the end of the chapter to determine how much you could have "saved" in overwithholding last year, or if you want to use the optional worksheets to determine how much you might "save" this year.

Note: *If you are not interested in making calculations or in learning how to compute the withholding amounts, you should skip the section in Appendix 1 and proceed directly to Example 1 on the following page.*

The examples shown next concern employees on monthly payroll periods. This was done for ease of demonstration, but the cumulative-wages method can also be used for employees on *any* payroll period.

Example 1

David and Mary are married, have two children, and are entitled to claim only four withholding allowances. Mary did not work in 1984, and she and David have no itemized deductions in excess of their zero bracket amount. David is paid monthly.

From January 1 through September 30, 1984, David earned $2,500 a month. Starting October 1 he got a promotion with a raise to $4,000 a month. His withholding for the year, using the wage bracket table would be:

```
Income  . . . . . . . . . . . . $2,500.00 × 9 mos = $22,500
Withholding  . . . . . . . $  338.80 × 9      = . . . . . . . . $3,049.20
Income  . . . . . . . . . . . . $4,000.00 × 3 mos =   12,000
Withholding  . . . . . . . $  798.90 × 3      = . . . . . . . .  2,396.70
    Total Income  . . . . . . . . . . . . . . . . . . . . . . . $34,500
    Total Withholding  . . . . . . . . . . . . . . . . . . . . . . . . . $5,445.90
```

David and Mary planned to file jointly and their tax liability was estimated as follows:

```
Income  . . . . . . . . . . . . . $34,500
Adjusted gross income .   34,500
Less excess itemized
    deductions  . . . . . . . . −    0
Less four exemptions    −4,000
Taxable income  =  . . . . $30,500
Tax liability  =  . . . . . . $  4,958.00 (1984 tax schedules)
Withholding  =  . . . . . . − 5,445.90 (1984 wage bracket table)
Overwithheld &
    refund  =  . . . . . . . . $    487.90
```

David then decided to ask his employer to use the cumulative-wages method, beginning when his income increased dramatically. To find out how much less would be withheld under this method, review the computations on David's optional worksheet on the following page.

CUMULATIVE WAGES METHOD

FOUR-STEP OPTIONAL WORKSHEET FOR EXAMPLE 1—DAVID: 1984

PAYROLL PERIOD	OCT. (#10)	NOV. (#11)	DEC. (#12)	
STEP 1: Enter the wages to be paid you for the current payroll period	$ 4,000	$ 4,000	$ 4,000	$ ____
Add the total wages already paid you during this calendar year by same employer	+22,500	+26,500	+30,500	+ ____
Equals	26,500	30,500	34,500	= ____
STEP 2: Divide the Step 1 amount by the total number of payroll periods used in Step 1: ÷ ____ =	$2,650	= $2,772.73	= $2,875	= ____
STEP 3: Find the tax that would have been withheld on the Step 2 amount using the percentage method*	376.26	407.88	436.52	____
Multiply by the total number of payroll periods used in Step 1	× 10	× 11	× 12	× ____
Equals	= 3,762.60	= 4,486.68	= 5,238.24	= ____
STEP 4: Subtract from the Step 3 amount the total tax already withheld during the calendar year	−3,049.20	−3,762.60	−4,486.73	− ____
This is the amount to be withheld	= $713.40	= $724.13	= $751.51	= ____

*When using the percentage method you must be careful to use the correct table. Write here the applicable:

Payroll Period _____

Marital Status _____

Number of Allowances Claimed _____

If you are claiming less than 9 allowances you can use the tables in Appendix 1 titled: "Wage Bracket Percentage Method Table for Computing Income Tax Withholding from Gross Wages."

If you are claiming more than 9 allowances you must use the method explained on pages 96–109, with the tables in Appendix 1 titled: "Percentage Method Withholding Computation."

David's total withholding under the cumulative-wages method is $5,238.24:

Withholding .... $338.80 × 9 = $3,049.20
Withholding using cumulative-wages method:

Oct.	713.40
Nov.	724.13
Dec.	751.51

Total withholding $5,238.24

Using the cumulative wages method, David was able to reduce his withholding by $207.66. This may not seem like much, but considering that the method was only used three times, the efforts could be considered worthwhile. Also, it should be pointed out that David was able to reduce his *overwithholding* from $487.90 (withholding of $5,445.90 using the wage bracket table less tax liability of $4,958) to $280.24 (withholding of $5,238.24 under the cumulative-wages method less tax liability of $4,958), a reduction of 42.5 percent of his overwithheld tax.

On the previous page and on the following page are two different worksheets for David's example, the Four-Step Optional Worksheet and the Summary Worksheet.

Note: *If you are not interested in making calculations or in learning how to compute the withholding amounts, proceed directly to Example 2.*

The Four-Step Optional Worksheet shows the computational process involved when using the cumulative-wages method. If you are now sure that you understand the computational process used in the cumulative-wages method, you should take the time to compare the information provided in the previous pages. This is necessary before proceeding with Example 2.

The Summary Worksheet chart for the cumulative-wages method using David's example is shown on page 102. Even though the worksheet may look ominous at first glance, it is not difficult to use. It is actually only a horizontal layout, across the page, of the Four-Step Optional Worksheet where the computations go down the page.

CUMULATIVE WAGES METHOD

SUMMARY WORKSHEET OF EXAMPLE 1—DAVID: 1984

	STEP 1		STEP 2		STEP 3		STEP 4		OPTIONAL
	(a)	(b)	(c)	(d)	(e)	(f)	(g)	(h)	(i)
Year: 1984	Income	Cumulative Wages	Payroll Period	Average Wages (b)÷(c)	Withholding on Column (d)— Percentage Method*	Cumulative Withholding (e)×(c)	Amount Already Withheld	Amount To Withhold (f)−(g)	Amount That Would Have Been Withheld**
JAN	$2,500.00	X	1	X	X	X	X	X	$ 338.80
FEB	2,500.00	X	2	X	X	X	X	X	338.80
MAR	2,500.00	X	3	X	X	X	X	X	338.80
APR	2,500.00	X	4	X	X	X	X	X	338.80
MAY	2,500.00	X	5	X	X	X	X	X	338.80
JUN	2,500.00	X	6	X	X	X	X	X	338.80
JUL	2,500.00	X	7	X	X	X	X	X	338.80
AUG	2,500.00	X	8	X	X	X	X	X	338.80
SEP	2,500.00	22,500.00	9	2,500.00	X	X	X	X	338.80
OCT	4,000.00	26,500.00	10	2,650.00	376.26	3,762.60	− 3,049.20***	713.40	798.90
NOV	4,000.00	30,500.00	11	2,772.73	407.88	4,486.73	− 3,762.60	724.13	798.90
DEC	4,000.00	34,500.00	12	2,875.00	436.52	5,238.24	− 4,486.73	751.51	798.90
TOTAL						5,238.24			5,445.90

*Column (e) must be computed using the percentage method. For this example you should use the Wage Bracket Percentage Method Table for Computing Income Tax Withholding From Gross Wages.

**Using wage bracket tables: This column is optional and not used in computations of the cumulative-wages method.

***This amount is the sum total of the withholding through the previous pay periods as occurred with the wage bracket tables.

The Summary Worksheet combines the methodology used in the Four-Step approach with the information of David's previous payroll periods to achieve a more comprehensive picture of David's withholding for the entire year. The layout of the Summary Worksheet chart allows you to more easily see the advantages of the cumulative-wages method and to compare the withholding amounts to what would otherwise be withheld without using the method.

Example 2

Lonnie and Barbara are married and have two children. They have large itemized deductions, tax credits, and four dependents. They are entitled to claim a total of eight withholding allowances: Barbara claims four allowances on her income and Lonnie claims four allowances on his income.

Lonnie is a commissioned salesman for a telecommunications equipment company. His income is erratic and subject to rather dramatic increases and decreases. In 1983 he earned $30,000, but because his employer withholds his taxes by using the wage bracket tables, Lonnie and Barbara were overwithheld $650.

Lonnie decided that he did not want to be overwithheld that much in 1984, so he requested his employer to use the cumulative-wages method instead of the wage bracket table method. He made his request in writing and submitted it by December 1, 1983. His employer began using the cumulative-wages method at the beginning of the first payroll period in 1984.

Lonnie's employer had to make a separate computation each month, but by the end of the year Lonnie had "saved" $291.86 in withholding taxes. The summary worksheet chart on the following page shows his monthly commission checks [column (a)] and the amount withheld under the cumulative-wages method [column (h)]. The differences in withholding amounts between the cumulative-wages method and the wage bracket table method are easily compared; column (i) shows the amounts that would have been withheld under the wage bracket table method.

CUMULATIVE WAGES METHOD

SUMMARY WORKSHEET OF EXAMPLE 2—LONNIE (MARRIED, MONTHLY, FOUR ALLOWANCES): 1984

| Year: 1984 | Step 1 | | Step 2 | | Step 3 | | Step 4 | | Optional |
	(a) Income	(b) Cumulative Wages	(c) Payroll Period	(d) Average Wages (b)÷(c)	(e) Withholding on Column (d)—Percentage Method	(f) Cumulative Withholding (e)×(c)	(g) Amount Already Withheld	(h) Amount To Withhold (f)−(g)	(i) Amount That Would Have Been Withheld
JAN	$1,750.00	$1,750.00	1	$1,750.00	$176.84	$176.84	$ -0- =	$ 176.84	$ 175.10
FEB	920.00	2,670.00	2	1,335.00	106.29	212.58	−176.84 =	35.74	209.60
MAR	3,350.00	6,020.00	3	2,006.67	224.31	672.93	−212.58 =	460.35	298.80
APR	1,580.00	7,600.00	4	1,900.00	202.34	809.36	−672.93 =	136.43	147.90
MAY	2,205.00	9,805.00	5	1,961.00	214.19	1,070.95	−809.36 =	261.59	271.20
JUN	1,110.00	10,915.00	6	1,819.17	188.57	1,131.42	−1,070.95 =	60.47	68.00
JUL	1,765.00	12,680.00	7	1,811.43	187.21	1,310.47	−1,131.42 =	179.05	181.90
AUG	2,180.00	14,860.00	8	1,857.50	195.20	1,561.60	−1,310.47 =	251.13	262.40
SEP	3,770.00	18,630.00	9	2,070.00	238.17	2,143.53	−1,561.60 =	581.93	719.70
OCT	2,215.00	20,845.00	10	2,084.50	241.47	2,414.70	−2,143.53 =	271.17	271.20
NOV	2,630.00	23,475.00	11	2,134.09	252.25	2,774.75	−2,414.70 =	360.05	378.80
DEC	3,580.00	27,055.00	12	2,254.58	278.87	3,346.44	−2,774.75 =	571.69	652.70
TOTAL						$3,346.44		$3,346.44	$3,638.30

INSTRUCTIONS FOR USE OF YOUR OPTIONAL WORKSHEETS—CUMULATIVE-WAGES METHOD

You may want to use the optional worksheets that follow:

- If you would like to recompute your withholding for last year to determine how much you would have "saved" had your employer used the cumulative-wages method. (For this you will need to contact the IRS or your employer for copies of last year's withholding tables for your marital status and payroll period.) This may influence your decision to ask your employer to change your withholding this year to the cumulative-wages method.

- If your income is consistent in amount each payroll period, but you are going to get a large increase in salary and would like to determine how much withholding you will "save" this year by using the cumulative-wages method.

Obviously, if your income fluctuates dramatically from pay period to pay period, you cannot reasonably estimate what your income will be in the future. But this worksheet may still be useful to you.

Remember: *Your employer computes your tax withholding. It is not necessary that you understand how the computations are made, nor is it necessary for you to use the optional worksheets. You only need to know that the cumulative-wages method is available and that it may "save" you money on your withholding taxes.*

For those who prefer the Four-Step Optional Worksheet as used in Example 1, the following pages are provided for your use. This format can be expanded on additional paper all the way up to fifty-two payroll periods, should you require them.

For those who understand the cumulative-wages method clearly and can use the Summary Worksheet, it is on pages 108–109. The Summary Worksheet chart can also be expanded up to 52 payroll periods very easily by simply adding another sheet of paper.

CUMULATIVE

FOUR-STEP OPTIONAL

PAYROLL PERIOD	1
STEP 1: Enter the wages to be paid you for the current payroll period	$_____
Add the total wages already paid you during this calendar year by same employer	+_____
Equals	=_____
STEP 2: Divide the Step 1 amount by the total number of payroll periods used in Step 1: _____ ÷ _____	= _____
STEP 3: Find the tax that would have been withheld on the Step 2 amount using the percentage method*	_____
Multiply by the total number of payroll periods used in Step 1	×_____
Equals	= _____
STEP 4: Subtract from the Step 3 amount the total tax already withheld during the calendar year	−_____
This is the amount to be withheld	= _____

*When using the percentage method you must be careful to use the correct table.
Write here the applicable:
    Payroll Period _____
    Marital Status _____
    Number of Allowances Claimed _____
If you are claiming less than 9 allowances you can use the tables in Appendix 1 titled: "Wage Bracket Percentage Method Table for Computing Income Tax Withholding from Gross Wages."
If you are claiming more than 9 allowances you must use the method explained on pages 96–109, with the tables in Appendix 1 titled: "Percentage Method Withholding Computation."

WAGES METHOD

WORKSHEET FOR YOU

2	3	4
$_____	$_____	$_____
+_____	+_____	+_____
=_____	=_____	=_____
_____	_____	_____
_____	_____	_____
×_____	×_____	×_____
=_____	=_____	=_____
−_____	−_____	−_____
=_____	=_____	=_____

CUMULATIVE

SUMMARY

Year	Step 1		Step 2	
	(a) Income	(b) Cumula-tive Wages	(c) Payroll Period	(d) Average Wages (b) ÷ (c)
			1	
			2	
			3	
			4	
			5	
			6	
			7	
			8	
			9	
			10	
			11	
			12	
			13	
			14	
			15	
			16	
			17	
			18	
			19	
			20	
			21	
			22	
			23	
			24	

WAGES METHOD

WORKSHEET FOR YOU

Step 3		Step 4		Optional
(e)	(f)	(g)	(h)	(i)
Withholding on Column (d)— Percentage Method	Cumulative Withholding (e) × (c)	Amount Already Withheld	Amount To Withhold (f) − (g)	Amount That Would Have Been Withheld
			−	=
			−	=
			−	=
			−	=
			−	=
			−	=
			−	=
			−	=
			−	=
			−	=
			−	=
			−	=
			−	=
			−	=
			−	=
			−	=
			−	=
			−	=
			−	=
			−	=
			−	=
			−	=
			−	=

Appendix 1: 1985 Withholding Tables

INTRODUCTION TO THE BASIC WITHHOLDING TABLES

Wage Bracket Tables

This is probably the most popular and common method for non-computerized payrolls. The IRS publishes withholding tables in IRS Publication 15, "Employer's Tax Guide" (also known as Circular E), that are set up by marital status (single or married) and payroll periods up to monthly. No computational work is required. All the employer has to do is look down the column to find the amount of wages being paid, and then go across the page to find the correct amount to be withheld under the column listing the number of withholding allowances claimed by his employee. The tables are quick and easy to use, and most small businesses use them. The complete set of wage bracket tables are on pages 112 through 131.

Percentage Method Tables

This method is probably the easiest for a computerized payroll system and must be used by employers with a quarterly, semiannual, or annual payroll period. The first step begins by subtracting an amount equivalent to each $1,040-per-year exemption (prorated for the pay period, e.g., $20.00 per week per one allowance) from the gross income earned, and then using special percentage tables to compute the amount to be withheld. The percentage tables are set up for particular payroll periods (e.g., weekly, biweekly, semimonthly, monthly, etc.) and then subdivided for the marital status of the employee.

There are several variations of the basic *percentage method*:

- *Alternative Formula Percentage Tables* IRS Publication 493 gives two alternative methods of computation that are especially designed for automated payroll systems. After subtracting the exempt allowance amount from the income earned, as is done in the basic percentage method, the method of computation is changed for the alternative formulas, making them easier to use in making computations. The alternative formulas can be used by several simple calculations on a pocket calculator without having to resort to making additional calculations off to the side or in the calculator's memory. Since the alternative formulas produce the exact same results as the percentage method tables, we will be using the Alternative 1 Table for the percentage method withholding computation when using withholding exemptions in excess of nine. A full explanation of how to use this table follows later.

- *Wage Bracket Percentage Method Tables* for automated payroll systems are also given in IRS Publication 493. There are two sets of withholding tables that are combinations of the wage bracket and alternative formula percentage method tables. The table labeled **"Wage Bracket Percentage Method Table for Computing INCOME TAX WITHHOLDING FROM GROSS WAGES"** is actually the easiest percentage method table to use up to nine withholding allowances. Like the alternative formula percentage method tables, the wage bracket percentage method tables can be used very easily with a pocket calculator; and because they have additional columns for up to nine withholding allowances, there is one less mathematical step involved in using them.

Guidelines on using the percentage method appear on pages 132–135. Percentage method tables appear on pages 136–141.

SINGLE Persons–WEEKLY Payroll Period
(For Wages Paid After December 1984)

And the wages are–		And the number of withholding allowances claimed is–										
At least	But less than	0	1	2	3	4	5	6	7	8	9	10
		The amount of income tax to be withheld shall be–										
$0	$30	$0	$0	$0	$0	$0	$0	$0	$0	$0	$0	$0
30	32	1	0	0	0	0	0	0	0	0	0	0
32	34	1	0	0	0	0	0	0	0	0	0	0
34	36	1	0	0	0	0	0	0	0	0	0	0
36	38	1	0	0	0	0	0	0	0	0	0	0
38	40	1	0	0	0	0	0	0	0	0	0	0
40	42	2	0	0	0	0	0	0	0	0	0	0
42	44	2	0	0	0	0	0	0	0	0	0	0
44	46	2	0	0	0	0	0	0	0	0	0	0
46	48	2	0	0	0	0	0	0	0	0	0	0
48	50	3	0	0	0	0	0	0	0	0	0	0
50	52	3	1	0	0	0	0	0	0	0	0	0
52	54	3	1	0	0	0	0	0	0	0	0	0
54	56	3	1	0	0	0	0	0	0	0	0	0
56	58	4	1	0	0	0	0	0	0	0	0	0
58	60	4	1	0	0	0	0	0	0	0	0	0
60	62	4	2	0	0	0	0	0	0	0	0	0
62	64	4	2	0	0	0	0	0	0	0	0	0
64	66	4	2	0	0	0	0	0	0	0	0	0
66	68	5	2	0	0	0	0	0	0	0	0	0
68	70	5	3	0	0	0	0	0	0	0	0	0
70	72	5	3	1	0	0	0	0	0	0	0	0
72	74	6	3	1	0	0	0	0	0	0	0	0
74	76	6	3	1	0	0	0	0	0	0	0	0
76	78	6	4	1	0	0	0	0	0	0	0	0
78	80	6	4	1	0	0	0	0	0	0	0	0
80	82	7	4	2	0	0	0	0	0	0	0	0
82	84	7	4	2	0	0	0	0	0	0	0	0
84	86	7	4	2	0	0	0	0	0	0	0	0
86	88	7	5	2	0	0	0	0	0	0	0	0
88	90	8	5	3	0	0	0	0	0	0	0	0
90	92	8	5	3	1	0	0	0	0	0	0	0
92	94	8	6	3	1	0	0	0	0	0	0	0
94	96	9	6	3	1	0	0	0	0	0	0	0
96	98	9	6	4	1	0	0	0	0	0	0	0
98	100	9	6	4	1	0	0	0	0	0	0	0
100	105	10	7	4	2	0	0	0	0	0	0	0
105	110	10	8	5	2	0	0	0	0	0	0	0
110	115	11	8	5	3	1	0	0	0	0	0	0
115	120	12	9	6	4	1	0	0	0	0	0	0
120	125	13	10	7	4	2	0	0	0	0	0	0
125	130	13	10	8	5	2	0	0	0	0	0	0
130	135	14	11	8	5	3	1	0	0	0	0	0
135	140	15	12	9	6	4	1	0	0	0	0	0
140	145	16	13	10	7	4	2	0	0	0	0	0
145	150	16	13	10	8	5	2	0	0	0	0	0
150	160	18	14	11	9	6	3	1	0	0	0	0
160	170	19	16	13	10	7	4	2	0	0	0	0
170	180	21	18	14	11	9	6	3	1	0	0	0
180	190	22	19	16	13	10	7	4	2	0	0	0
190	200	24	21	18	14	11	9	6	3	1	0	0
200	210	26	22	19	16	13	10	7	4	2	0	0
210	220	27	24	21	18	14	11	9	6	3	1	0
220	230	29	26	22	19	16	13	10	7	4	2	0
230	240	31	27	24	21	18	14	11	9	6	3	1
240	250	33	29	26	22	19	16	13	10	7	4	2
250	260	35	31	27	24	21	18	14	11	9	6	3
260	270	37	33	29	26	22	19	16	13	10	7	4
270	280	39	35	31	27	24	21	18	14	11	9	6
280	290	41	37	33	29	26	22	19	16	13	10	7
290	300	43	39	35	31	27	24	21	18	14	11	9
300	310	46	41	37	33	29	26	22	19	16	13	10
310	320	48	43	39	35	31	27	24	21	18	14	11
320	330	50	46	41	37	33	29	26	22	19	16	13
330	340	53	48	43	39	35	31	27	24	21	18	14
340	350	55	50	46	41	37	33	29	26	22	19	16
350	360	58	53	48	43	39	35	31	27	24	21	18
360	370	60	55	50	46	41	37	33	29	26	22	19
370	380	63	58	53	48	43	39	35	31	27	24	21

(Continued on next page)

SINGLE Persons–WEEKLY Payroll Period
(For Wages Paid After December 1984)

And the wages are–		And the number of withholding allowances claimed is–										
At least	But less than	0	1	2	3	4	5	6	7	8	9	10
		The amount of income tax to be withheld shall be–										
$380	$390	$65	$60	$55	$50	$46	$41	$37	$33	$29	$26	$22
390	400	68	63	58	53	48	43	39	35	31	27	24
400	410	71	65	60	55	50	46	41	37	33	29	26
410	420	73	68	63	58	53	48	43	39	35	31	27
420	430	76	71	65	60	55	50	46	41	37	33	29
430	440	78	73	68	63	58	53	48	43	39	35	31
440	450	81	76	71	65	60	55	50	46	41	37	33
450	460	84	78	73	68	63	58	53	48	43	39	35
460	470	87	81	76	71	65	60	55	50	46	41	37
470	480	90	84	78	73	68	63	58	53	48	43	39
480	490	93	87	81	76	71	65	60	55	50	46	41
490	500	96	90	84	78	73	68	63	58	53	48	43
500	510	99	93	87	81	76	71	65	60	55	50	46
510	520	102	96	90	84	78	73	68	63	58	53	48
520	530	105	99	93	87	81	76	71	65	60	55	50
530	540	108	102	96	90	84	78	73	68	63	58	53
540	550	111	105	99	93	87	81	76	71	65	60	55
550	560	114	108	102	96	90	84	78	73	68	63	58
560	570	117	111	105	99	93	87	81	76	71	65	60
570	580	121	114	108	102	96	90	84	78	73	68	63
580	590	124	117	111	105	99	93	87	81	76	71	65
590	600	127	121	114	108	102	96	90	84	78	73	68
600	610	131	124	117	111	105	99	93	87	81	76	71
610	620	134	127	121	114	108	102	96	90	84	78	73
620	630	138	131	124	117	111	105	99	93	87	81	76
630	640	141	134	127	121	114	108	102	96	90	84	78
640	650	144	138	131	124	117	111	105	99	93	87	81
650	660	148	141	134	127	121	114	108	102	96	90	84
660	670	151	144	138	131	124	117	111	105	99	93	87
670	680	155	148	141	134	127	121	114	108	102	96	90
680	690	159	151	144	138	131	124	117	111	105	99	93
690	700	162	155	148	141	134	127	121	114	108	102	96
700	710	166	159	151	144	138	131	124	117	111	105	99
710	720	170	162	155	148	141	134	127	121	114	108	102
720	730	173	166	159	151	144	138	131	124	117	111	105
730	740	177	170	162	155	148	141	134	127	121	114	108
740	750	181	173	166	159	151	144	138	131	124	117	111
750	760	184	177	170	162	155	148	141	134	127	121	114
760	770	188	181	173	166	159	151	148	138	131	124	117
770	780	192	184	177	170	162	155	148	141	134	127	121
780	790	196	188	181	173	166	159	151	144	138	131	124
790	800	199	192	184	177	170	162	155	148	141	134	127
800	810	203	196	188	181	173	166	159	151	144	138	131
810	820	207	199	192	184	177	170	162	155	148	141	134
820	830	210	203	196	188	181	173	166	159	151	144	138
830	840	214	207	199	192	184	177	170	162	155	148	141
840	850	218	210	203	196	188	181	173	166	159	151	144
850	860	221	214	207	199	192	184	177	170	162	155	148
860	870	225	218	210	203	196	188	181	173	166	159	151
870	880	229	221	214	207	199	192	184	177	170	162	155
880	890	233	225	218	210	203	196	188	181	173	166	159
890	900	236	229	221	214	207	199	192	184	177	170	162
900	910	240	233	225	218	210	203	196	188	181	173	166
910	920	244	236	229	221	214	207	199	192	184	177	170
920	930	247	240	233	225	218	210	203	196	188	181	173
930	940	251	244	236	229	221	214	207	199	192	184	177
940	950	255	247	240	233	225	218	210	203	196	188	181
950	960	258	251	244	236	229	221	214	207	199	192	184
960	970	262	255	247	240	233	225	218	210	203	196	188
970	980	266	258	251	244	236	229	221	214	207	199	192
980	990	270	262	255	247	240	233	225	218	210	203	196
990	1,000	273	266	258	251	244	236	229	221	214	207	199
1,000	1,010	277	270	262	255	247	240	233	225	218	210	203
1,010	1,020	281	273	266	258	251	244	236	229	221	214	207
1,020	1,030	284	277	270	262	255	247	240	233	225	218	210
37 percent of the excess over $1,030 plus–												
$1,030 and over		286	279	271	264	257	249	242	234	227	220	212

MARRIED Persons–WEEKLY Payroll Period
(For Wages Paid After December 1984)

And the wages are–		And the number of withholding allowances claimed is–										
At least	But less than	0	1	2	3	4	5	6	7	8	9	10
		The amount of income tax to be withheld shall be–										
$0	$52	$0	$0	$0	$0	$0	$0	$0	$0	$0	$0	$0
52	54	1	0	0	0	0	0	0	0	0	0	0
54	56	1	0	0	0	0	0	0	0	0	0	0
56	58	1	0	0	0	0	0	0	0	0	0	0
58	60	1	0	0	0	0	0	0	0	0	0	0
60	62	1	0	0	0	0	0	0	0	0	0	0
62	64	2	0	0	0	0	0	0	0	0	0	0
64	66	2	0	0	0	0	0	0	0	0	0	0
66	68	2	0	0	0	0	0	0	0	0	0	0
68	70	2	0	0	0	0	0	0	0	0	0	0
70	72	3	0	0	0	0	0	0	0	0	0	0
72	74	3	1	0	0	0	0	0	0	0	0	0
74	76	3	1	0	0	0	0	0	0	0	0	0
76	78	3	1	0	0	0	0	0	0	0	0	0
78	80	3	1	0	0	0	0	0	0	0	0	0
80	82	4	1	0	0	0	0	0	0	0	0	0
82	84	4	2	0	0	0	0	0	0	0	0	0
84	86	4	2	0	0	0	0	0	0	0	0	0
86	88	4	2	0	0	0	0	0	0	0	0	0
88	90	5	2	0	0	0	0	0	0	0	0	0
90	92	5	3	0	0	0	0	0	0	0	0	0
92	94	5	3	1	0	0	0	0	0	0	0	0
94	96	5	3	1	0	0	0	0	0	0	0	0
96	98	5	3	1	0	0	0	0	0	0	0	0
98	100	6	3	1	0	0	0	0	0	0	0	0
100	105	6	4	2	0	0	0	0	0	0	0	0
105	110	7	4	2	0	0	0	0	0	0	0	0
110	115	7	5	3	0	0	0	0	0	0	0	0
115	120	8	6	3	1	0	0	0	0	0	0	0
120	125	9	6	4	2	0	0	0	0	0	0	0
125	130	9	7	4	2	0	0	0	0	0	0	0
130	135	10	7	5	3	0	0	0	0	0	0	0
135	140	10	8	6	3	1	0	0	0	0	0	0
140	145	11	9	6	4	2	0	0	0	0	0	0
145	150	12	9	7	4	2	0	0	0	0	0	0
150	160	13	10	8	5	3	1	0	0	0	0	0
160	170	14	11	9	6	4	2	0	0	0	0	0
170	180	16	13	10	8	5	3	1	0	0	0	0
180	190	17	14	11	9	6	4	2	0	0	0	0
190	200	18	16	13	10	8	5	3	1	0	0	0
200	210	20	17	14	11	9	6	4	2	0	0	0
210	220	21	18	16	13	10	8	5	3	1	0	0
220	230	23	20	17	14	11	9	6	4	2	0	0
230	240	24	21	18	16	13	10	8	5	3	1	0
240	250	26	23	20	17	14	11	9	6	4	2	0
250	260	28	24	21	18	16	13	10	8	5	3	1
260	270	29	26	23	20	17	14	11	9	6	4	2
270	280	31	28	24	21	18	16	13	10	8	5	3
280	290	32	29	26	23	20	17	14	11	9	6	4
290	300	34	31	28	24	21	18	16	13	10	8	5
300	310	36	32	29	26	23	20	17	14	11	9	6
310	320	38	34	31	28	24	21	18	16	13	10	8
320	330	39	36	32	29	26	23	20	17	14	11	9
330	340	41	38	34	31	28	24	21	18	16	13	10
340	350	43	39	36	32	29	26	23	20	17	14	11
350	360	45	41	38	34	31	28	24	21	18	16	13
360	370	47	43	39	36	32	29	26	23	20	17	14
370	380	48	45	41	38	34	31	28	24	21	18	16
380	390	50	47	43	39	36	32	29	26	23	20	17
390	400	52	48	45	41	38	34	31	28	24	21	18
400	410	55	50	47	43	39	36	32	29	26	23	20
410	420	57	52	48	45	41	38	34	31	28	24	21
420	430	59	55	50	47	43	39	36	32	29	26	23
430	440	61	57	52	48	45	41	38	34	31	28	24
440	450	63	59	55	50	47	43	39	36	32	29	26
450	460	66	61	57	52	48	45	41	38	34	31	28
460	470	68	63	59	55	50	47	43	39	36	32	29
470	480	70	66	61	57	52	48	45	41	38	34	31
480	490	73	68	63	59	55	50	47	43	39	36	32

(Continued on next page)

MARRIED Persons–WEEKLY Payroll Period
(For Wages Paid After December 1984)

And the wages are–		And the number of withholding allowances claimed is–										
At least	But less than	0	1	2	3	4	5	6	7	8	9	10
		The amount of income tax to be withheld shall be–										
$490	$500	$75	$70	$66	$61	$57	$52	$48	$45	$41	$38	$34
500	510	78	73	68	63	59	55	50	47	43	39	36
510	520	80	75	70	66	61	57	52	48	45	41	38
520	530	83	78	73	68	63	59	55	50	47	43	39
530	540	85	80	75	70	66	61	57	52	48	45	41
540	550	88	83	78	73	68	63	59	55	50	47	43
550	560	90	85	80	75	70	66	61	57	52	48	45
560	570	93	88	83	78	73	68	63	59	55	50	47
570	580	95	90	85	80	75	70	66	61	57	52	48
580	590	98	93	88	83	78	73	68	63	59	55	50
590	600	101	95	90	85	80	75	70	66	61	57	52
600	610	103	98	93	88	83	78	73	68	63	59	55
610	620	106	101	95	90	85	80	75	70	66	61	57
620	630	109	103	98	93	88	83	78	73	68	63	59
630	640	112	106	101	95	90	85	80	75	70	66	61
640	650	115	109	103	98	93	88	83	78	73	68	63
650	660	117	112	106	101	95	90	85	80	75	70	66
660	670	120	115	109	103	98	93	88	83	78	73	68
670	680	123	117	112	106	101	95	90	85	80	75	70
680	690	126	120	115	109	103	98	93	88	83	78	73
690	700	129	123	117	112	106	101	95	90	85	80	75
700	710	132	126	120	115	109	103	98	93	88	83	78
710	720	136	129	123	117	112	106	101	95	90	85	80
720	730	139	132	126	120	115	109	103	98	93	88	83
730	740	142	136	129	123	117	112	106	101	95	90	85
740	750	146	139	132	126	120	115	109	103	98	93	88
750	760	149	142	136	129	123	117	112	106	101	95	90
760	770	152	146	139	132	126	120	115	109	103	98	93
770	780	155	149	142	136	129	123	117	112	106	101	95
780	790	159	152	146	139	132	126	120	115	109	103	98
790	800	162	155	149	142	136	129	123	117	112	106	101
800	810	165	159	152	146	139	132	126	120	115	109	103
810	820	169	162	155	149	142	136	129	123	117	112	106
820	830	172	165	159	152	146	139	132	126	120	115	109
830	840	175	169	162	155	149	142	136	129	123	117	112
840	850	179	172	165	159	152	146	139	132	126	120	115
850	860	182	175	169	162	155	149	142	136	129	123	117
860	870	185	179	172	165	159	152	146	139	132	126	120
870	880	188	182	175	169	162	155	149	142	136	129	123
880	890	192	185	179	172	165	159	152	146	139	132	126
890	900	195	188	182	175	169	162	155	149	142	136	129
900	910	199	192	185	179	172	165	159	152	146	139	132
910	920	202	195	188	182	175	169	162	155	149	142	136
920	930	206	199	192	185	179	172	165	159	152	146	139
930	940	210	202	195	188	182	175	169	162	155	149	142
940	950	213	206	199	192	185	179	172	165	159	152	146
950	960	217	210	202	195	188	182	175	169	162	155	149
960	970	221	213	206	199	192	185	179	172	165	159	152
970	980	225	217	210	202	195	188	182	175	169	162	155
980	990	228	221	213	206	199	192	185	179	172	165	159
990	1,000	232	225	217	210	202	195	188	182	175	169	162
1,000	1,010	236	228	221	213	206	199	192	185	179	172	165
1,010	1,020	239	232	225	217	210	202	195	188	182	175	169
1,020	1,030	243	236	228	221	213	206	199	192	185	179	172
1,030	1,040	247	239	232	225	217	210	202	195	188	182	175
1,040	1,050	250	243	236	228	221	213	206	199	192	185	179
1,050	1,060	254	247	239	232	225	217	210	202	195	188	182
1,060	1,070	258	250	243	236	228	221	213	206	199	192	185
1,070	1,080	262	254	247	239	232	225	217	210	202	195	188
1,080	1,090	265	258	250	243	236	228	221	213	206	199	192
1,090	1,100	269	262	254	247	239	232	225	217	210	202	195
1,100	1,110	273	265	258	250	243	236	228	221	213	206	199
1,110	1,120	276	269	262	254	247	239	232	225	217	210	202
1,120	1,130	280	273	265	258	250	243	236	228	221	213	206
1,130	1,140	284	276	269	262	254	247	239	232	225	217	210
		37 percent of the excess over $1,140 plus–										
$1,140 and over		286	278	271	263	256	249	241	234	226	219	212

SINGLE Persons–BIWEEKLY Payroll Period
(For Wages Paid After December 1984)

And the wages are–		And the number of withholding allowances claimed is–										
At least	But less than	0	1	2	3	4	5	6	7	8	9	10
		The amount of income tax to be withheld shall be–										
$0	$56	$0	$0	$0	$0	$0	$0	$0	$0	$0	$0	$0
56	58	1	0	0	0	0	0	0	0	0	0	0
58	60	1	0	0	0	0	0	0	0	0	0	0
60	62	1	0	0	0	0	0	0	0	0	0	0
62	64	1	0	0	0	0	0	0	0	0	0	0
64	66	1	0	0	0	0	0	0	0	0	0	0
66	68	2	0	0	0	0	0	0	0	0	0	0
68	70	2	0	0	0	0	0	0	0	0	0	0
70	72	2	0	0	0	0	0	0	0	0	0	0
72	74	2	0	0	0	0	0	0	0	0	0	0
74	76	3	0	0	0	0	0	0	0	0	0	0
76	78	3	0	0	0	0	0	0	0	0	0	0
78	80	3	0	0	0	0	0	0	0	0	0	0
80	82	3	0	0	0	0	0	0	0	0	0	0
82	84	3	0	0	0	0	0	0	0	0	0	0
84	86	4	0	0	0	0	0	0	0	0	0	0
86	88	4	0	0	0	0	0	0	0	0	0	0
88	90	4	0	0	0	0	0	0	0	0	0	0
90	92	4	0	0	0	0	0	0	0	0	0	0
92	94	5	0	0	0	0	0	0	0	0	0	0
94	96	5	0	0	0	0	0	0	0	0	0	0
96	98	5	1	0	0	0	0	0	0	0	0	0
98	100	5	1	0	0	0	0	0	0	0	0	0
100	102	5	1	0	0	0	0	0	0	0	0	0
102	104	6	1	0	0	0	0	0	0	0	0	0
104	106	6	1	0	0	0	0	0	0	0	0	0
106	108	6	2	0	0	0	0	0	0	0	0	0
108	110	6	2	0	0	0	0	0	0	0	0	0
110	112	7	2	0	0	0	0	0	0	0	0	0
112	114	7	2	0	0	0	0	0	0	0	0	0
114	116	7	3	0	0	0	0	0	0	0	0	0
116	118	7	3	0	0	0	0	0	0	0	0	0
118	120	8	3	0	0	0	0	0	0	0	0	0
120	124	8	3	0	0	0	0	0	0	0	0	0
124	128	8	4	0	0	0	0	0	0	0	0	0
128	132	9	4	0	0	0	0	0	0	0	0	0
132	136	9	5	0	0	0	0	0	0	0	0	0
136	140	10	5	1	0	0	0	0	0	0	0	0
140	144	10	6	1	0	0	0	0	0	0	0	0
144	148	11	6	2	0	0	0	0	0	0	0	0
148	152	12	7	2	0	0	0	0	0	0	0	0
152	156	12	7	2	0	0	0	0	0	0	0	0
156	160	13	7	3	0	0	0	0	0	0	0	0
160	164	13	8	3	0	0	0	0	0	0	0	0
164	168	14	8	4	0	0	0	0	0	0	0	0
168	172	14	9	4	0	0	0	0	0	0	0	0
172	176	15	9	5	0	0	0	0	0	0	0	0
176	180	16	10	5	1	0	0	0	0	0	0	0
180	184	16	10	6	1	0	0	0	0	0	0	0
184	188	17	11	6	2	0	0	0	0	0	0	0
188	192	17	12	7	2	0	0	0	0	0	0	0
192	196	18	12	7	2	0	0	0	0	0	0	0
196	200	18	13	7	3	0	0	0	0	0	0	0
200	210	19	14	8	4	0	0	0	0	0	0	0
210	220	21	15	10	5	0	0	0	0	0	0	0
220	230	22	17	11	6	1	0	0	0	0	0	0
230	240	24	18	12	7	3	0	0	0	0	0	0
240	250	25	19	14	8	4	0	0	0	0	0	0
250	260	27	21	15	10	5	0	0	0	0	0	0
260	270	28	22	17	11	6	1	0	0	0	0	0
270	280	30	24	18	12	7	3	0	0	0	0	0
280	290	31	25	19	14	8	4	0	0	0	0	0
290	300	33	27	21	15	10	5	0	0	0	0	0
300	320	35	29	23	17	12	7	2	0	0	0	0
320	340	38	32	26	20	14	9	4	0	0	0	0
340	360	41	35	29	23	17	12	7	2	0	0	0
360	380	45	38	32	26	20	14	9	4	0	0	0
380	400	48	41	35	29	23	17	12	7	2	0	0
400	420	51	45	38	32	26	20	14	9	4	0	0
420	440	55	48	41	35	29	23	17	12	7	2	0

(Continued on next page)

SINGLE Persons–BIWEEKLY Payroll Period
(For Wages Paid After December 1984)

And the wages are–		And the number of withholding allowances claimed is–										
At least	But less than	0	1	2	3	4	5	6	7	8	9	10
		The amount of income tax to be withheld shall be–										
$440	$460	$59	$51	$45	$38	$32	$26	$20	$14	$9	$4	$0
460	480	62	55	48	41	35	29	23	17	12	7	2
480	500	66	59	51	45	38	32	26	20	14	9	4
500	520	70	62	55	48	41	35	29	23	17	12	7
520	540	74	66	59	51	45	38	32	26	20	14	9
540	560	78	70	62	55	48	41	35	29	23	17	12
560	580	82	74	66	59	51	45	38	32	26	20	14
580	600	87	78	70	62	55	48	41	35	29	23	17
600	620	92	82	74	66	59	51	45	38	32	26	20
620	640	96	87	78	70	62	55	48	41	35	29	23
640	660	101	92	82	74	66	59	51	45	38	32	26
660	680	105	96	87	78	70	62	55	48	41	35	29
680	700	110	101	92	82	74	66	59	51	45	38	32
700	720	115	105	96	87	78	70	62	55	48	41	35
720	740	120	110	101	92	82	74	66	59	51	45	38
740	760	126	115	105	96	87	78	70	62	55	48	41
760	780	131	120	110	101	92	82	74	66	59	51	45
780	800	136	126	115	105	96	87	78	70	62	55	48
800	820	141	131	120	110	101	92	82	74	66	59	51
820	840	146	136	126	115	105	96	87	78	70	62	55
840	860	152	141	131	120	110	101	92	82	74	66	59
860	880	157	146	136	126	115	105	96	87	78	70	62
880	900	162	152	141	131	120	110	101	92	82	74	66
900	920	168	157	146	136	126	115	105	96	87	78	70
920	940	174	162	152	141	131	120	110	101	92	82	74
940	960	180	168	157	146	136	126	115	105	96	87	78
960	980	186	174	162	152	141	131	120	110	101	92	82
980	1,000	192	180	168	157	146	136	126	115	105	96	87
1,000	1,020	198	186	174	162	152	141	131	120	110	101	92
1,020	1,040	204	192	180	168	157	146	136	126	115	105	96
1,040	1,060	210	198	186	174	162	152	141	131	120	110	101
1,060	1,080	216	204	192	180	168	157	146	136	126	115	105
1,080	1,100	222	210	198	186	174	162	152	141	131	120	110
1,100	1,120	228	216	204	192	180	168	157	146	136	126	115
1,120	1,140	234	222	210	198	186	174	162	152	141	131	120
1,140	1,160	241	228	216	204	192	180	168	157	146	136	126
1,160	1,180	248	234	222	210	198	186	174	162	152	141	131
1,180	1,200	255	241	228	216	204	192	180	168	157	146	136
1,200	1,220	261	248	234	222	210	198	186	174	162	152	141
1,220	1,240	268	255	241	228	216	204	192	180	168	157	146
1,240	1,260	275	261	248	234	222	210	198	186	174	162	152
1,260	1,280	282	268	255	241	228	216	204	192	180	168	157
1,280	1,300	289	275	261	248	234	222	210	198	186	174	162
1,300	1,320	295	282	268	255	241	228	216	204	192	180	168
1,320	1,340	302	289	275	261	248	234	222	210	198	186	174
1,340	1,360	310	295	282	268	255	241	228	216	204	192	180
1,360	1,380	317	302	289	275	261	248	234	222	210	198	186
1,380	1,400	325	310	295	282	268	255	241	228	216	204	192
1,400	1,420	332	317	302	289	275	261	248	234	222	210	198
1,420	1,440	339	325	310	295	282	268	255	241	228	216	204
1,440	1,460	347	332	317	302	289	275	261	248	234	222	210
1,460	1,480	354	339	325	310	295	282	268	255	241	228	216
1,480	1,500	362	347	332	317	302	289	275	261	248	234	222
1,500	1,520	369	354	339	325	310	295	282	268	255	241	228
1,520	1,540	376	362	347	332	317	302	289	275	261	248	234
1,540	1,560	384	369	354	339	325	310	295	282	268	255	241
1,560	1,580	391	376	362	347	332	317	302	289	275	261	248
1,580	1,600	399	384	369	354	339	325	310	295	282	268	255
1,600	1,620	406	391	376	362	347	332	317	302	289	275	261
1,620	1,640	413	399	384	369	354	339	325	310	295	282	268
1,640	1,660	421	406	391	376	362	347	332	317	302	289	275
1,660	1,680	428	413	399	384	369	354	339	325	310	295	282
1,680	1,700	436	421	406	391	376	362	347	332	317	302	289
1,700	1,720	443	428	413	399	384	369	354	339	325	310	295
1,720	1,740	450	436	421	406	391	376	362	347	332	317	302
		37 percent of the excess over $1,740 plus–										
$1,740 and over		454	439	424	410	395	380	365	350	336	321	306

MARRIED Persons–BIWEEKLY Payroll Period
(For Wages Paid After December 1984)

And the wages are–		And the number of withholding allowances claimed is–										
At least	But less than	0	1	2	3	4	5	6	7	8	9	10
		The amount of income tax to be withheld shall be–										
$0	$100	$0	$0	$0	$0	$0	$0	$0	$0	$0	$0	$0
100	102	1	0	0	0	0	0	0	0	0	0	0
102	104	1	0	0	0	0	0	0	0	0	0	0
104	106	1	0	0	0	0	0	0	0	0	0	0
106	108	1	0	0	0	0	0	0	0	0	0	0
108	110	1	0	0	0	0	0	0	0	0	0	0
110	112	2	0	0	0	0	0	0	0	0	0	0
112	114	2	0	0	0	0	0	0	0	0	0	0
114	116	2	0	0	0	0	0	0	0	0	0	0
116	118	2	0	0	0	0	0	0	0	0	0	0
118	120	3	0	0	0	0	0	0	0	0	0	0
120	124	3	0	0	0	0	0	0	0	0	0	0
124	128	3	0	0	0	0	0	0	0	0	0	0
128	132	4	0	0	0	0	0	0	0	0	0	0
132	136	4	0	0	0	0	0	0	0	0	0	0
136	140	5	0	0	0	0	0	0	0	0	0	0
140	144	5	1	0	0	0	0	0	0	0	0	0
144	148	5	1	0	0	0	0	0	0	0	0	0
148	152	6	2	0	0	0	0	0	0	0	0	0
152	156	6	2	0	0	0	0	0	0	0	0	0
156	160	7	2	0	0	0	0	0	0	0	0	0
160	164	7	3	0	0	0	0	0	0	0	0	0
164	168	8	3	0	0	0	0	0	0	0	0	0
168	172	8	4	0	0	0	0	0	0	0	0	0
172	176	9	4	0	0	0	0	0	0	0	0	0
176	180	9	5	0	0	0	0	0	0	0	0	0
180	184	9	5	1	0	0	0	0	0	0	0	0
184	188	10	5	1	0	0	0	0	0	0	0	0
188	192	10	6	2	0	0	0	0	0	0	0	0
192	196	11	6	2	0	0	0	0	0	0	0	0
196	200	11	7	2	0	0	0	0	0	0	0	0
200	210	12	8	3	0	0	0	0	0	0	0	0
210	220	13	9	4	0	0	0	0	0	0	0	0
220	230	15	10	5	1	0	0	0	0	0	0	0
230	240	16	11	6	2	0	0	0	0	0	0	0
240	250	17	12	8	3	0	0	0	0	0	0	0
250	260	18	13	9	4	0	0	0	0	0	0	0
260	270	19	15	10	5	1	0	0	0	0	0	0
270	280	21	16	11	6	2	0	0	0	0	0	0
280	290	22	17	12	8	3	0	0	0	0	0	0
290	300	24	18	13	9	4	0	0	0	0	0	0
300	320	26	20	15	10	6	2	0	0	0	0	0
320	340	29	23	18	13	8	4	0	0	0	0	0
340	360	31	26	20	15	10	6	2	0	0	0	0
360	380	34	29	23	18	13	8	4	0	0	0	0
380	400	37	31	26	20	15	10	6	2	0	0	0
400	420	40	34	29	23	18	13	8	4	0	0	0
420	440	43	37	31	26	20	15	10	6	2	0	0
440	460	46	40	34	29	23	18	13	8	4	0	0
460	480	49	43	37	31	26	20	15	10	6	2	0
480	500	52	46	40	34	29	23	18	13	8	4	0
500	520	55	49	43	37	31	26	20	15	10	6	2
520	540	58	52	46	40	34	29	23	18	13	8	4
540	560	62	55	49	43	37	31	26	20	15	10	6
560	580	65	58	52	46	40	34	29	23	18	13	8
580	600	68	62	55	49	43	37	31	26	20	15	10
600	620	71	65	58	52	46	40	34	29	23	18	13
620	640	75	68	62	55	49	43	37	31	26	20	15
640	660	79	71	65	58	52	46	40	34	29	23	18
660	680	82	75	68	62	55	49	43	37	31	26	20
680	700	86	79	71	65	58	52	46	40	34	29	23
700	720	89	82	75	68	62	55	49	43	37	31	26
720	740	93	86	79	71	65	58	52	46	40	34	29
740	760	97	89	82	75	68	62	55	49	43	37	31
760	780	100	93	86	79	71	65	58	52	46	40	34
780	800	105	97	89	82	75	68	62	55	49	43	37
800	820	109	100	93	86	79	71	65	58	52	46	40
820	840	113	105	97	89	82	75	68	62	55	49	43
840	860	118	109	100	93	86	79	71	65	58	52	46
860	880	122	113	105	97	89	82	75	68	62	55	49
880	900	127	118	109	100	93	86	79	71	65	58	52

(Continued on next page)

MARRIED Persons–BIWEEKLY Payroll Period
(For Wages Paid After December 1984)

At least	But less than	0	1	2	3	4	5	6	7	8	9	10
$900	$920	$131	$122	$113	$105	$97	$89	$82	$75	$68	$62	$55
920	940	135	127	118	109	100	93	86	79	71	65	58
940	960	140	131	122	113	105	97	89	82	75	68	62
960	980	145	135	127	118	109	100	93	86	79	71	65
980	1,000	150	140	131	122	113	105	97	89	82	75	68
1,000	1,020	155	145	135	127	118	109	100	93	86	79	71
1,020	1,040	160	150	140	131	122	113	105	97	89	82	75
1,040	1,060	165	155	145	135	127	118	109	100	93	86	79
1,060	1,080	170	160	150	140	131	122	113	105	97	89	82
1,080	1,100	175	165	155	145	135	127	118	109	100	93	86
1,100	1,120	180	170	160	150	140	131	122	113	105	97	89
1,120	1,140	185	175	165	155	145	135	127	118	109	100	93
1,140	1,160	190	180	170	160	150	140	131	122	113	105	97
1,160	1,180	195	185	175	165	155	145	135	127	118	109	100
1,180	1,200	201	190	180	170	160	150	140	131	122	113	105
1,200	1,220	207	195	185	175	165	155	145	135	127	118	109
1,220	1,240	212	201	190	180	170	160	150	140	131	122	113
1,240	1,260	218	207	195	185	175	165	155	145	135	127	118
1,260	1,280	223	212	201	190	180	170	160	150	140	131	122
1,280	1,300	229	218	207	195	185	175	165	155	145	135	127
1,300	1,320	235	223	212	201	190	180	170	160	150	140	131
1,320	1,340	240	229	218	207	195	185	175	165	155	145	135
1,340	1,360	246	235	223	212	201	190	180	170	160	150	140
1,360	1,380	251	240	229	218	207	195	185	175	165	155	145
1,380	1,400	258	246	235	223	212	201	190	180	170	160	150
1,400	1,420	265	251	240	229	218	207	195	185	175	165	155
1,420	1,440	271	258	246	235	223	212	201	190	180	170	160
1,440	1,460	278	265	251	240	229	218	207	195	185	175	165
1,460	1,480	284	271	258	246	235	223	212	201	190	180	170
1,480	1,500	291	278	265	251	240	229	218	207	195	185	175
1,500	1,520	298	284	271	258	246	235	223	212	201	190	180
1,520	1,540	304	291	278	265	251	240	229	218	207	195	185
1,540	1,560	311	298	284	271	258	246	235	223	212	201	190
1,560	1,580	317	304	291	278	265	251	240	229	218	207	195
1,580	1,600	324	311	298	284	271	258	246	235	223	212	201
1,600	1,620	331	317	304	291	278	265	251	240	229	218	207
1,620	1,640	337	324	311	298	284	271	258	246	235	223	212
1,640	1,660	344	331	317	304	291	278	265	251	240	229	218
1,660	1,680	350	337	324	311	298	284	271	258	246	235	223
1,680	1,700	357	344	331	317	304	291	278	265	251	240	229
1,700	1,720	364	350	337	324	311	298	284	271	258	246	235
1,720	1,740	370	357	344	331	317	304	291	278	265	251	240
1,740	1,760	377	364	350	337	324	311	298	284	271	258	246
1,760	1,780	383	370	357	344	331	317	304	291	278	265	251
1,780	1,800	390	377	364	350	337	324	311	298	284	271	258
1,800	1,820	397	383	370	357	344	331	317	304	291	278	265
1,820	1,840	405	390	377	364	350	337	324	311	298	284	271
1,840	1,860	412	397	383	370	357	344	331	317	304	291	278
1,860	1,880	420	405	390	377	364	350	337	324	311	298	284
1,880	1,900	427	412	397	383	370	357	344	331	317	304	291
1,900	1,920	434	420	405	390	377	364	350	337	324	311	298
1,920	1,940	442	427	412	397	383	370	357	344	331	317	304
1,940	1,960	449	434	420	405	390	377	364	350	337	324	311
1,960	1,980	457	442	427	412	397	383	370	357	344	331	317
1,980	2,000	464	449	434	420	405	390	377	364	350	337	324
2,000	2,020	471	457	442	427	412	397	383	370	357	344	331
2,020	2,040	479	464	449	434	420	405	390	377	364	350	337
2,040	2,060	486	471	457	442	427	412	397	383	370	357	344
2,060	2,080	494	479	464	449	434	420	405	390	377	364	350
2,080	2,100	501	486	471	457	442	427	412	397	383	370	357
2,100	2,120	508	494	479	464	449	434	420	405	390	377	364
2,120	2,140	516	501	486	471	457	442	427	412	397	383	370
2,140	2,160	523	508	494	479	464	449	434	420	405	390	377
2,160	2,180	531	516	501	486	471	457	442	427	412	397	383
2,180	2,200	538	523	508	494	479	464	449	434	420	405	390
2,200	2,220	545	531	516	501	486	471	457	442	427	412	397
37 percent of the excess over $2,220 plus–												
$2,220 and over		549	534	519	505	490	475	460	445	431	416	401

SINGLE Persons–SEMIMONTHLY Payroll Period
(For Wages Paid After December 1984)

At least	But less than	0	1	2	3	4	5	6	7	8	9	10
\$0	\$60	\$0	\$0	\$0	\$0	\$0	\$0	\$0	\$0	\$0	\$0	\$0
60	62	1	0	0	0	0	0	0	0	0	0	0
62	64	1	0	0	0	0	0	0	0	0	0	0
64	66	1	0	0	0	0	0	0	0	0	0	0
66	68	1	0	0	0	0	0	0	0	0	0	0
68	70	1	0	0	0	0	0	0	0	0	0	0
70	72	2	0	0	0	0	0	0	0	0	0	0
72	74	2	0	0	0	0	0	0	0	0	0	0
74	76	2	0	0	0	0	0	0	0	0	0	0
76	78	2	0	0	0	0	0	0	0	0	0	0
78	80	3	0	0	0	0	0	0	0	0	0	0
80	82	3	0	0	0	0	0	0	0	0	0	0
82	84	3	0	0	0	0	0	0	0	0	0	0
84	86	3	0	0	0	0	0	0	0	0	0	0
86	88	3	0	0	0	0	0	0	0	0	0	0
88	90	4	0	0	0	0	0	0	0	0	0	0
90	92	4	0	0	0	0	0	0	0	0	0	0
92	94	4	0	0	0	0	0	0	0	0	0	0
94	96	4	0	0	0	0	0	0	0	0	0	0
96	98	4	0	0	0	0	0	0	0	0	0	0
98	100	5	0	0	0	0	0	0	0	0	0	0
100	102	5	0	0	0	0	0	0	0	0	0	0
102	104	5	0	0	0	0	0	0	0	0	0	0
104	106	5	1	0	0	0	0	0	0	0	0	0
106	108	6	1	0	0	0	0	0	0	0	0	0
108	110	6	1	0	0	0	0	0	0	0	0	0
110	112	6	1	0	0	0	0	0	0	0	0	0
112	114	6	1	0	0	0	0	0	0	0	0	0
114	116	7	2	0	0	0	0	0	0	0	0	0
116	118	7	2	0	0	0	0	0	0	0	0	0
118	120	7	2	0	0	0	0	0	0	0	0	0
120	124	7	2	0	0	0	0	0	0	0	0	0
124	128	8	3	0	0	0	0	0	0	0	0	0
128	132	8	3	0	0	0	0	0	0	0	0	0
132	136	9	4	0	0	0	0	0	0	0	0	0
136	140	9	4	0	0	0	0	0	0	0	0	0
140	144	10	5	0	0	0	0	0	0	0	0	0
144	148	10	5	0	0	0	0	0	0	0	0	0
148	152	11	6	1	0	0	0	0	0	0	0	0
152	156	11	6	1	0	0	0	0	0	0	0	0
156	160	12	7	2	0	0	0	0	0	0	0	0
160	164	13	7	2	0	0	0	0	0	0	0	0
164	168	13	7	3	0	0	0	0	0	0	0	0
168	172	14	8	3	0	0	0	0	0	0	0	0
172	176	14	8	3	0	0	0	0	0	0	0	0
176	180	15	9	4	0	0	0	0	0	0	0	0
180	184	15	9	4	0	0	0	0	0	0	0	0
184	188	16	10	5	0	0	0	0	0	0	0	0
188	192	16	10	5	0	0	0	0	0	0	0	0
192	196	17	11	6	1	0	0	0	0	0	0	0
196	200	18	11	6	1	0	0	0	0	0	0	0
200	210	19	12	7	2	0	0	0	0	0	0	0
210	220	20	14	8	3	0	0	0	0	0	0	0
220	230	21	15	9	4	0	0	0	0	0	0	0
230	240	23	17	11	5	1	0	0	0	0	0	0
240	250	24	18	12	7	2	0	0	0	0	0	0
250	260	26	19	13	8	3	0	0	0	0	0	0
260	270	27	21	15	9	4	0	0	0	0	0	0
270	280	29	22	16	10	5	0	0	0	0	0	0
280	290	30	24	18	12	6	1	0	0	0	0	0
290	300	32	25	19	13	7	2	0	0	0	0	0
300	320	34	27	21	15	9	4	0	0	0	0	0
320	340	37	30	24	18	12	6	2	0	0	0	0
340	360	40	33	27	21	15	9	4	0	0	0	0
360	380	43	36	30	23	17	11	6	1	0	0	0
380	400	47	40	33	26	20	14	8	3	0	0	0
400	420	50	43	36	29	23	17	11	6	1	0	0
420	440	53	46	39	32	26	20	14	8	3	0	0
440	460	57	49	42	35	29	22	16	10	5	0	0
460	480	60	52	46	39	32	25	19	13	8	3	0
480	500	64	56	49	42	35	28	22	16	10	5	0
500	520	67	60	52	45	38	31	25	19	13	7	2

(Continued on next page)

SINGLE Persons–SEMIMONTHLY Payroll Period
(For Wages Paid After December 1984)

And the wages are–		And the number of withholding allowances claimed is–										
At least	But less than	0	1	2	3	4	5	6	7	8	9	10
		The amount of income tax to be withheld shall be–										
$520	$540	$71	$63	$55	$48	$41	$34	$28	$22	$15	$10	$4
540	560	75	67	59	51	44	38	31	24	18	12	7
560	580	79	71	63	55	48	41	34	27	21	15	9
580	600	83	75	66	58	51	44	37	30	24	18	12
600	620	87	79	70	62	54	47	40	33	27	21	15
620	640	92	83	74	66	58	50	43	36	30	23	17
640	660	97	87	78	69	61	54	47	40	33	26	20
660	680	101	91	82	73	65	57	50	43	36	29	23
680	700	106	96	86	77	69	61	53	46	39	32	26
700	720	110	100	91	81	73	64	57	49	42	35	29
720	740	115	105	95	85	77	68	60	52	46	39	32
740	760	120	110	100	90	81	72	64	56	49	42	35
760	780	125	114	104	94	85	76	67	60	52	45	38
780	800	130	119	109	99	89	80	71	63	55	48	41
800	820	135	124	114	104	94	84	75	67	59	51	44
820	840	141	129	118	108	98	88	79	71	63	55	48
840	860	146	135	123	113	103	93	83	75	66	58	51
860	880	151	140	128	117	107	97	87	79	70	62	54
880	900	156	145	134	122	112	102	92	83	74	66	58
900	920	161	150	139	128	117	107	97	87	78	69	61
920	940	167	155	144	133	122	111	101	91	82	73	65
940	960	172	161	149	138	127	116	106	96	86	77	69
960	980	177	166	154	143	132	121	110	100	91	81	73
980	1,000	183	171	160	148	137	126	115	105	95	85	77
1,000	1,020	189	176	165	154	142	131	120	110	100	90	81
1,020	1,040	195	182	170	159	148	136	125	114	104	94	85
1,040	1,060	201	188	175	164	153	141	130	119	109	99	89
1,060	1,080	207	194	181	169	158	147	135	124	114	104	94
1,080	1,100	213	200	187	174	163	152	141	129	118	108	98
1,100	1,120	219	206	193	180	168	157	146	135	123	113	103
1,120	1,140	225	212	199	186	174	162	151	140	128	117	107
1,140	1,160	231	218	205	192	179	167	156	145	134	122	112
1,160	1,180	237	224	211	198	185	173	161	150	139	128	117
1,180	1,200	243	230	217	204	191	178	167	155	144	133	122
1,200	1,220	249	236	223	210	197	184	172	161	149	138	127
1,220	1,240	256	242	229	216	203	190	177	166	154	143	132
1,240	1,260	263	248	235	222	209	196	183	171	160	148	137
1,260	1,280	269	255	241	228	215	202	189	176	165	154	142
1,280	1,300	276	261	247	234	221	208	195	182	170	159	148
1,300	1,320	283	268	253	240	227	214	201	188	175	164	153
1,320	1,340	290	275	260	246	233	220	207	194	181	169	158
1,340	1,360	297	282	267	252	239	226	213	200	187	174	163
1,360	1,380	303	289	274	259	245	232	219	206	193	180	168
1,380	1,400	310	295	281	266	251	238	225	212	199	186	174
1,400	1,420	317	302	287	273	258	244	231	218	205	192	179
1,420	1,440	324	309	294	280	265	250	237	224	211	198	185
1,440	1,460	331	316	301	286	272	257	243	230	217	204	191
1,460	1,480	338	323	308	293	278	264	249	236	223	210	197
1,480	1,500	346	330	315	300	285	270	256	242	229	216	203
1,500	1,520	353	337	321	307	292	277	263	248	235	222	209
1,520	1,540	361	345	328	314	299	284	269	255	241	228	215
1,540	1,560	368	352	336	320	306	291	276	261	247	234	221
1,560	1,580	375	359	343	327	312	298	283	268	253	240	227
1,580	1,600	383	367	351	335	319	304	290	275	260	246	233
1,600	1,620	390	374	358	342	326	311	297	282	267	252	239
1,620	1,640	398	382	365	349	333	318	303	289	274	259	245
1,640	1,660	405	389	373	357	341	325	310	295	281	266	251
1,660	1,680	412	396	380	364	348	332	317	302	287	273	258
1,680	1,700	420	404	388	372	356	340	324	309	294	280	265
1,700	1,720	427	411	395	379	363	347	331	316	301	286	272
1,720	1,740	435	419	402	386	370	354	338	323	308	293	278
1,740	1,760	442	426	410	394	378	362	346	330	315	300	285
1,760	1,780	449	433	417	401	385	369	353	337	321	307	292
1,780	1,800	457	441	425	409	393	377	361	345	328	314	299
1,800	1,820	464	448	432	416	400	384	368	352	336	320	306
1,820	1,840	472	456	439	423	407	391	375	359	343	327	312
1,840	1,860	479	463	447	431	415	399	383	367	351	335	319
1,860	1,880	486	470	454	438	422	406	390	374	358	342	326
		37 percent of the excess over $1,880 plus–										
$1,880 and over		490	474	458	442	426	410	394	378	362	346	330

MARRIED Persons–SEMIMONTHLY Payroll Period

(For Wages Paid After December 1984)

And the wages are–		And the number of withholding allowances claimed is–										
At least	But less than	0	1	2	3	4	5	6	7	8	9	10
		The amount of income tax to be withheld shall be–										
$0	$108	$0	$0	$0	$0	$0	$0	$0	$0	$0	$0	$0
108	110	1	0	0	0	0	0	0	0	0	0	0
110	112	1	0	0	0	0	0	0	0	0	0	0
112	114	1	0	0	0	0	0	0	0	0	0	0
114	116	1	0	0	0	0	0	0	0	0	0	0
116	118	1	0	0	0	0	0	0	0	0	0	0
118	120	2	0	0	0	0	0	0	0	0	0	0
120	124	2	0	0	0	0	0	0	0	0	0	0
124	128	2	0	0	0	0	0	0	0	0	0	0
128	132	3	0	0	0	0	0	0	0	0	0	0
132	136	3	0	0	0	0	0	0	0	0	0	0
136	140	4	0	0	0	0	0	0	0	0	0	0
140	144	4	0	0	0	0	0	0	0	0	0	0
144	148	5	0	0	0	0	0	0	0	0	0	0
148	152	5	0	0	0	0	0	0	0	0	0	0
152	156	5	1	0	0	0	0	0	0	0	0	0
156	160	6	1	0	0	0	0	0	0	0	0	0
160	164	6	2	0	0	0	0	0	0	0	0	0
164	168	7	2	0	0	0	0	0	0	0	0	0
168	172	7	2	0	0	0	0	0	0	0	0	0
172	176	8	3	0	0	0	0	0	0	0	0	0
176	180	8	3	0	0	0	0	0	0	0	0	0
180	184	9	4	0	0	0	0	0	0	0	0	0
184	188	9	4	0	0	0	0	0	0	0	0	0
188	192	9	5	0	0	0	0	0	0	0	0	0
192	196	10	5	0	0	0	0	0	0	0	0	0
196	200	10	6	1	0	0	0	0	0	0	0	0
200	210	11	6	2	0	0	0	0	0	0	0	0
210	220	12	7	3	0	0	0	0	0	0	0	0
220	230	14	9	4	0	0	0	0	0	0	0	0
230	240	15	10	5	0	0	0	0	0	0	0	0
240	250	16	11	6	1	0	0	0	0	0	0	0
250	260	17	12	7	2	0	0	0	0	0	0	0
260	270	18	13	8	3	0	0	0	0	0	0	0
270	280	20	14	9	4	0	0	0	0	0	0	0
280	290	21	16	10	6	1	0	0	0	0	0	0
290	300	22	17	12	7	2	0	0	0	0	0	0
300	320	24	19	13	8	4	0	0	0	0	0	0
320	340	27	21	16	11	6	1	0	0	0	0	0
340	360	30	24	18	13	8	3	0	0	0	0	0
360	380	33	27	21	15	10	5	1	0	0	0	0
380	400	35	29	23	18	13	8	3	0	0	0	0
400	420	38	32	26	20	15	10	5	0	0	0	0
420	440	41	35	29	23	17	12	7	2	0	0	0
440	460	44	38	32	26	20	15	9	5	0	0	0
460	480	47	41	35	28	22	17	12	7	2	0	0
480	500	50	43	37	31	25	19	14	9	4	0	0
500	520	53	46	40	34	28	22	17	12	7	2	0
520	540	56	49	43	37	31	25	19	14	9	4	0
540	560	59	52	46	40	34	28	21	16	11	6	1
560	580	63	56	49	42	36	30	24	19	13	8	4
580	600	66	59	52	45	39	33	27	21	16	11	6
600	620	69	62	55	48	42	36	30	24	18	13	8
620	640	72	65	58	51	45	39	33	27	21	15	10
640	660	75	68	62	55	48	42	35	29	23	18	13
660	680	79	72	65	58	51	44	38	32	26	20	15
680	700	83	75	68	61	54	47	41	35	29	23	17
700	720	86	78	71	64	57	50	44	38	32	26	20
720	740	90	82	74	67	60	54	47	41	35	28	22
740	760	93	86	78	71	64	• 57	50	43	37	31	25
760	780	97	89	81	74	67	60	53	46	40	34	28
780	800	101	93	85	77	70	63	56	49	43	37	31
800	820	104	96	89	81	73	66	59	52	46	40	34
820	840	108	100	92	84	77	70	63	56	49	43	36
840	860	112	104	96	88	80	73	66	59	52	45	39
860	880	117	107	99	92	84	76	69	62	55	48	42
880	900	121	111	103	95	87	80	72	65	58	51	45
900	920	125	116	107	99	91	83	75	68	62	55	48
920	940	130	120	111	102	95	87	79	72	65	58	51
940	960	134	125	115	106	98	90	83	75	68	61	54
960	980	139	129	119	110	102	94	86	78	71	64	57
980	1,000	143	133	124	114	105	98	90	82	74	67	60
1,000	1,020	147	138	128	119	109	101	93	86	78	71	64

(Continued on next page)

MARRIED Persons–SEMIMONTHLY Payroll Period
(For Wages Paid After December 1984)

And the wages are–		And the number of withholding allowances claimed is–										
At least	But less than	0	1	2	3	4	5	6	7	8	9	10
		The amount of income tax to be withheld shall be–										
$1,020	$1,040	$152	$142	$133	$123	$114	$105	$97	$89	$81	$74	$67
1,040	1,060	157	147	137	128	118	108	101	93	85	77	70
1,060	1,080	162	151	141	132	122	113	104	96	89	81	73
1,080	1,100	167	156	146	136	127	117	108	100	92	84	77
1,100	1,120	172	161	150	141	131	122	112	104	96	88	80
1,120	1,140	177	166	155	145	136	126	117	107	99	92	84
1,140	1,160	182	171	160	150	140	130	121	111	103	95	87
1,160	1,180	187	176	165	154	144	135	125	116	107	99	91
1,180	1,200	192	181	170	159	149	139	130	120	111	102	95
1,200	1,220	197	186	175	164	154	144	134	125	115	106	98
1,220	1,240	202	191	180	169	159	148	139	129	119	110	102
1,240	1,260	207	196	185	174	164	153	143	133	124	114	105
1,260	1,280	212	201	190	179	169	158	147	138	128	119	109
1,280	1,300	218	206	195	184	174	163	152	142	133	123	114
1,300	1,320	224	211	200	189	179	168	157	147	137	128	118
1,320	1,340	229	217	205	194	184	173	162	151	141	132	122
1,340	1,360	235	223	211	199	189	178	167	156	146	136	127
1,360	1,380	240	228	216	204	194	183	172	161	150	141	131
1,380	1,400	246	234	222	210	199	188	177	166	155	145	136
1,400	1,420	252	239	227	215	204	193	182	171	160	150	140
1,420	1,440	257	245	233	221	209	198	187	176	165	154	144
1,440	1,460	263	251	239	226	214	203	192	181	170	159	149
1,460	1,480	268	256	244	232	220	208	197	186	175	164	154
1,480	1,500	274	262	250	238	225	213	202	191	180	169	159
1,500	1,520	281	267	255	243	231	219	207	196	185	174	164
1,520	1,540	288	273	261	249	237	225	212	201	190	179	169
1,540	1,560	294	280	267	254	242	230	218	206	195	184	174
1,560	1,580	301	286	272	260	248	236	224	211	200	189	179
1,580	1,600	307	293	279	266	253	241	229	217	205	194	184
1,600	1,620	314	300	285	271	259	247	235	223	211	199	189
1,620	1,640	321	306	292	278	265	253	240	228	216	204	194
1,640	1,660	327	313	299	284	270	258	246	234	222	210	199
1,660	1,680	334	319	305	291	277	264	252	239	227	215	204
1,680	1,700	340	326	312	297	283	269	257	245	233	221	209
1,700	1,720	347	333	318	304	290	275	263	251	239	226	214
1,720	1,740	354	339	325	311	296	282	268	256	244	232	220
1,740	1,760	360	346	332	317	303	289	274	262	250	238	225
1,760	1,780	367	352	338	324	310	295	281	267	255	243	231
1,780	1,800	373	359	345	330	316	302	288	273	261	249	237
1,800	1,820	380	366	351	337	323	308	294	280	267	254	242
1,820	1,840	387	372	358	344	329	315	301	286	272	260	248
1,840	1,860	393	379	365	350	336	322	307	293	279	266	253
1,860	1,880	400	385	371	357	343	328	314	300	285	271	259
1,880	1,900	406	392	378	363	349	335	321	306	292	278	265
1,900	1,920	413	399	384	370	356	341	327	313	299	284	270
1,920	1,940	420	405	391	377	362	348	334	319	305	291	277
1,940	1,960	426	412	398	383	369	355	340	326	312	297	283
1,960	1,980	434	418	404	390	376	361	347	333	318	304	290
1,980	2,000	441	425	411	396	382	368	354	339	325	311	296
2,000	2,020	449	433	417	403	389	374	360	346	332	317	303
2,020	2,040	456	440	424	410	395	381	367	352	338	324	310
2,040	2,060	463	447	431	416	402	388	373	359	345	330	316
2,060	2,080	471	455	439	423	409	394	380	366	351	337	323
2,080	2,100	478	462	446	430	415	401	387	372	358	344	329
2,100	2,120	486	470	454	438	422	407	393	379	365	350	336
2,120	2,140	493	477	461	445	429	414	400	385	371	357	343
2,140	2,160	500	484	468	452	436	421	406	392	378	363	349
2,160	2,180	508	492	476	460	444	428	413	399	384	370	356
2,180	2,200	515	499	483	467	451	435	420	405	391	377	362
2,200	2,220	523	507	491	475	459	442	426	412	398	383	369
2,220	2,240	530	514	498	482	466	450	434	418	404	390	376
2,240	2,260	537	521	505	489	473	457	441	425	411	396	382
2,260	2,280	545	529	513	497	481	465	449	433	417	403	389
2,280	2,300	552	536	520	504	488	472	456	440	424	410	395
2,300	2,320	560	544	528	512	496	479	463	447	431	416	402
2,320	2,340	567	551	535	519	503	487	471	455	439	423	409
2,340	2,360	574	558	542	526	510	494	478	462	446	430	415
2,360	2,380	582	566	550	534	518	502	486	470	454	438	422
2,380	2,400	589	573	557	541	525	509	493	477	461	445	429
		37 percent of the excess over $2,400 plus–										
$2,400 and over		593	577	561	545	529	513	497	481	465	449	433

SINGLE Persons—MONTHLY Payroll Period
(For Wages Paid After December 1984)

And the wages are—		And the number of withholding allowances claimed is—										
At least	But less than	0	1	2	3	4	5	6	7	8	9	10
		The amount of income tax to be withheld shall be—										
$0	$116	$0	$0	$0	$0	$0	$0	$0	$0	$0	$0	$0
116	120	1	0	0	0	0	0	0	0	0	0	0
120	124	1	0	0	0	0	0	0	0	0	0	0
124	128	1	0	0	0	0	0	0	0	0	0	0
128	132	2	0	0	0	0	0	0	0	0	0	0
132	136	2	0	0	0	0	0	0	0	0	0	0
136	140	3	0	0	0	0	0	0	0	0	0	0
140	144	3	0	0	0	0	0	0	0	0	0	0
144	148	4	0	0	0	0	0	0	0	0	0	0
148	152	4	0	0	0	0	0	0	0	0	0	0
152	156	5	0	0	0	0	0	0	0	0	0	0
156	160	5	0	0	0	0	0	0	0	0	0	0
160	164	5	0	0	0	0	0	0	0	0	0	0
164	168	6	0	0	0	0	0	0	0	0	0	0
168	172	6	0	0	0	0	0	0	.0	0	0	0	0
172	176	7	0	0	0	0	0	0	0	0	0	0
176	180	7	0	0	0	0	0	0	0	0	0	0
180	184	8	0	0	0	0	0	0	0	0	0	0
184	188	8	0	0	0	0	0	0	0	0	0	0
188	192	9	0	0	0	0	0	0	0	0	0	0
192	196	9	0	0	0	0	0	0	0	0	0	0
196	200	9	0	0	0	0	0	0	0	0	0	0
200	204	10	0	0	0	0	0	0	0	0	0	0
204	208	10	1	0	0	0	0	0	0	0	0	0
208	212	11	1	0	0	0	0	0	0	0	0	0
212	216	11	2	0	0	0	0	0	0	0	0	0
216	220	12	2	0	0	0	0	0	0	0	0	0
220	224	12	3	0	0	0	0	0	0	0	0	0
224	228	13	3	0	0	0	0	0	0	0	0	0
228	232	13	3	0	0	0	0	0	0	0	0	0
232	236	14	4	0	0	0	0	0	0	0	0	0
236	240	14	4	0	0	0	0	0	0	0	0	0
240	248	15	5	0	0	0	0	0	0	0	0	0
248	256	16	6	0	0	0	0	0	0	0	0	0
256	264	17	7	0	0	0	0	0	0	0	0	0
264	272	18	8	0	0	0	0	0	0	0	0	0
272	280	19	8	0	0	0	0	0	0	0	0	0
280	288	20	9	0	0	0	0	0	0	0	0	0
288	296	21	10	1	0	0	0	0	0	0	0	0
296	304	22	11	2	0	0	0	0	0	0	0	0
304	312	23	12	2	0	0	0	0	0	0	0	0
312	320	24	13	3	0	0	0	0	0	0	0	0
320	328	25	14	4	0	0	0	0	0	0	0	0
328	336	26	15	5	0	0	0	0	0	0	0	0
336	344	27	16	6	0	0	0	0	0	0	0	0
344	352	28	17	7	0	0	0	0	0	0	0	0
352	360	29	18	8	0	0	0	0	0	0	0	0
360	368	31	19	9	0	0	0	0	0	0	0	0
368	376	32	20	9	0	0	0	0	0	0	0	0
376	384	33	21	10	1	0	0	0	0	0	0	0
384	392	34	22	11	2	0	0	0	0	0	0	0
392	400	35	23	12	3	0	0	0	0	0	0	0
400	420	37	25	14	4	0	0	0	0	0	0	0
420	440	40	28	16	6	0	0	0	0	0	0	0
440	460	43	31	19	9	0	0	0	0	0	0	0
460	480	45	33	21	11	1	0	0	0	0	0	0
480	500	48	36	24	13	3	0	0	0	0	0	0
500	520	51	39	27	16	6	0	0	0	0	0	0
520	540	54	42	30	18	8	0	0	0	0	0	0
540	560	57	45	32	20	10	0	0	0	0	0	0
560	580	60	47	35	23	12	3	0	0	0	0	0
580	600	63	50	38	26	15	5	0	0	0	0	0
600	640	68	55	42	30	18	8	0	0	0	0	0
640	680	74	61	48	36	24	13	3	0	0	0	0
680	720	80	67	54	41	29	18	7	0	0	0	0
720	760	87	73	60	47	35	23	12	2	0	0	0
760	800	93	79	66	53	40	28	17	7	0	0	0
800	840	100	86	72	59	46	34	22	11	2	0	0
840	880	106	92	78	65	52	39	27	16	6	0	0
880	920	113	99	85	71	58	45	33	21	10	1	0
920	960	121	105	91	77	64	51	38	26	15	5	0
960	1,000	128	112	97	84	70	57	44	32	20	10	0
1,000	1,040	135	119	104	90	76	63	50	38	25	14	4

(Continued on next page)

SINGLE Persons—MONTHLY Payroll Period
(For Wages Paid After December 1984)

And the wages are—		And the number of withholding allowances claimed is—										
At least	But less than	0	1	2	3	4	5	6	7	8	9	10
		The amount of income tax to be withheld shall be—										
$1,040	$1,080	$143	$127	$111	$96	$83	$69	$56	$43	$31	$19	$9
1,080	1,120	151	134	118	103	89	75	62	49	37	24	14
1,120	1,160	159	141	125	110	95	81	68	55	42	30	18
1,160	1,200	167	149	133	117	102	88	74	61	48	36	24
1,200	1,240	175	157	140	124	109	94	80	67	54	41	29
1,240	1,280	184	165	148	131	116	101	87	73	60	47	35
1,280	1,320	193	173	156	139	123	107	93	79	66	53	40
1,320	1,360	202	183	164	147	130	115	100	86	72	59	46
1,360	1,400	212	192	172	155	137	122	106	92	78	65	52
1,400	1,440	221	201	181	163	145	129	113	99	85	71	58
1,440	1,480	230	210	190	171	153	136	121	105	91	77	64
1,480	1,520	240	219	199	179	161	144	128	112	97	84	70
1,520	1,560	250	229	209	189	169	152	135	119	104	90	76
1,560	1,600	260	238	218	198	178	160	143	127	111	96	83
1,600	1,640	271	248	227	207	187	168	151	134	118	103	89
1,640	1,680	281	259	236	216	196	176	159	141	125	110	95
1,680	1,720	292	269	246	225	206	186	167	149	133	117	102
1,720	1,760	302	279	257	235	215	195	175	157	140	124	109
1,760	1,800	312	290	267	245	224	204	184	165	148	131	116
1,800	1,840	323	300	278	255	233	213	193	173	156	139	123
1,840	1,880	333	311	288	266	243	222	202	183	164	147	130
1,880	1,920	344	321	298	276	253	232	212	192	172	155	137
1,920	1,960	354	331	309	286	264	241	221	201	181	163	145
1,960	2,000	365	342	319	297	274	252	230	210	190	171	153
2,000	2,040	377	352	330	307	285	262	240	219	199	179	161
2,040	2,080	389	363	340	318	295	272	250	229	209	189	169
2,080	2,120	401	375	350	328	305	283	260	238	218	198	178
2,120	2,160	413	387	361	338	316	293	271	248	227	207	187
2,160	2,200	425	399	373	349	326	304	281	259	236	216	196
2,200	2,240	437	411	385	359	337	314	292	269	246	225	206
2,240	2,280	449	423	397	371	347	324	302	279	257	235	215
2,280	2,320	461	435	409	383	357	335	312	290	267	245	224
2,320	2,360	473	447	421	395	369	345	323	300	278	255	233
2,360	2,400	485	459	433	407	381	356	333	311	288	266	243
2,400	2,440	498	471	445	419	393	367	344	321	298	276	253
2,440	2,480	511	483	457	431	405	379	354	331	309	286	264
2,480	2,520	525	496	469	443	417	391	365	342	319	297	274
2,520	2,560	539	509	481	455	429	403	377	352	330	307	285
2,560	2,600	552	523	493	467	441	415	389	363	340	318	295
2,600	2,640	566	536	507	479	453	427	401	375	350	328	305
2,640	2,680	579	550	521	491	465	439	413	387	361	338	316
2,680	2,720	593	564	534	505	477	451	425	399	373	349	326
2,720	2,760	607	577	548	518	489	463	437	411	385	359	337
2,760	2,800	620	591	561	532	502	475	449	423	397	371	347
2,800	2,840	634	604	575	545	516	487	461	435	409	383	357
2,840	2,880	647	618	589	559	530	500	473	447	421	395	369
2,880	2,920	662	632	602	573	543	514	485	459	433	407	381
2,920	2,960	677	645	616	586	557	527	498	471	445	419	393
2,960	3,000	692	659	629	600	570	541	511	483	457	431	405
3,000	3,040	706	674	643	613	584	555	525	496	469	443	417
3,040	3,080	721	689	657	627	598	568	539	509	481	455	429
3,080	3,120	736	704	672	641	611	582	552	523	493	467	441
3,120	3,160	751	719	687	655	625	595	566	536	507	479	453
3,160	3,200	766	733	701	669	638	609	579	550	521	491	465
3,200	3,240	780	748	716	684	652	623	593	564	534	505	477
3,240	3,280	795	763	731	699	667	636	607	577	548	518	489
3,280	3,320	810	778	746	714	682	650	620	591	561	532	502
3,320	3,360	825	793	761	729	696	664	634	604	575	545	516
3,360	3,400	840	807	775	743	711	679	647	618	589	559	530
3,400	3,440	854	822	790	758	726	694	662	632	602	573	543
3,440	3,480	869	837	805	773	741	709	677	645	616	586	557
3,480	3,520	884	852	820	788	756	724	692	659	629	600	570
3,520	3,560	899	867	835	803	770	738	706	674	643	613	584
3,560	3,600	914	881	849	817	785	753	721	689	657	627	598
3,600	3,640	928	896	864	832	800	768	736	704	672	641	611
3,640	3,680	943	911	879	847	815	783	751	719	687	655	625
3,680	3,720	958	926	894	862	830	798	766	733	701	669	638
3,720	3,760	973	941	909	877	844	812	780	748	716	684	652
		37 percent of the excess over $3,760 plus—										
$3,760 and over		980	948	916	884	852	820	788	756	724	692	659

MARRIED Persons—MONTHLY Payroll Period
(For Wages Paid After December 1984)

And the wages are—		And the number of withholding allowances claimed is—										
At least	But less than	0	1	2	3	4	5	6	7	8	9	10
		The amount of income tax to be withheld shall be—										
$0	$212	$0	$0	$0	$0	$0	$0	$0	$0	$0	$0	$0
212	216	1	0	0	0	0	0	0	0	0	0	0
216	220	1	0	0	0	0	0	0	0	0	0	0
220	224	2	0	0	0	0	0	0	0	0	0	0
224	228	2	0	0	0	0	0	0	0	0	0	0
228	232	2	0	0	0	0	0	0	0	0	0	0
232	236	3	0	0	0	0	0	0	0	0	0	0
236	240	3	0	0	0	0	0	0	0	0	0	0
240	248	4	0	0	0	0	0	0	0	0	0	0
248	256	5	0	0	0	0	0	0	0	0	0	0
256	264	6	0	0	0	0	0	0	0	0	0	0
264	272	7	0	0	0	0	0	0	0	0	0	0
272	280	7	0	0	0	0	0	0	0	0	0	0
280	288	8	0	0	0	0	0	0	0	0	0	0
288	296	9	0	0	0	0	0	0	0	0	0	0
296	304	10	1	0	0	0	0	0	0	0	0	0
304	312	11	1	0	0	0	0	0	0	0	0	0
312	320	12	2	0	0	0	0	0	0	0	0	0
320	328	13	3	0	0	0	0	0	0	0	0	0
328	336	14	4	0	0	0	0	0	0	0	0	0
336	344	14	5	0	0	0	0	0	0	0	0	0
344	352	15	6	0	0	0	0	0	0	0	0	0
352	350	16	7	0	0	0	0	0	0	0	0	0
360	368	17	8	0	0	0	0	0	0	0	0	0
368	376	18	8	0	0	0	0	0	0	0	0	0
376	384	19	9	0	0	0	0	0	0	0	0	0
384	392	20	10	1	0	0	0	0	0	0	0	0
392	400	21	11	2	0	0	0	0	0	0	0	0
400	420	22	13	3	0	0	0	0	0	0	0	0
420	440	25	15	5	0	0	0	0	0	0	0	0
440	460	27	17	8	0	0	0	0	0	0	0	0
460	480	30	19	10	0	0	0	0	0	0	0	0
480	500	32	22	12	2	0	0	0	0	0	0	0
500	520	34	24	14	5	0	0	0	0	0	0	0
520	540	37	26	16	7	0	0	0	0	0	0	0
540	560	39	29	19	9	0	0	0	0	0	0	0
560	580	42	31	21	11	2	0	0	0	0	0	0
580	600	44	34	23	13	4	0	0	0	0	0	0
600	640	49	37	27	17	7	0	0	0	0	0	0
640	680	54	42	32	21	12	2	0	0	0	0	0
680	720	60	48	36	26	16	6	0	0	0	0	0
720	760	65	53	41	31	20	11	1	0	0	0	0
760	800	71	59	47	36	25	15	6	0	0	0	0
800	840	77	64	52	40	30	20	10	1	0	0	0
840	880	82	70	58	46	35	24	14	5	0	0	0
880	920	88	76	63	51	40	29	19	9	0	0	0
920	960	93	81	69	57	45	34	24	14	4	0	0
960	1,000	100	87	75	63	50	39	28	18	9	0	0
1,000	1,040	106	92	80	68	56	44	33	23	13	3	0
1,040	1,080	112	99	86	74	62	49	38	28	17	8	0
1,080	1,120	119	105	91	79	67	55	43	32	22	12	3
1,120	1,160	125	111	98	85	73	61	49	37	27	17	7
1,160	1,200	132	118	104	91	78	66	54	42	32	21	12
1,200	1,240	138	124	110	96	84	72	60	48	36	26	16
1,240	1,280	144	131	117	103	90	77	65	53	41	31	20
1,280	1,320	151	137	123	109	95	83	71	59	47	36	25
1,320	1,360	158	143	130	116	102	89	77	64	52	40	30
1,360	1,400	165	150	136	122	108	94	82	70	58	46	35
1,400	1,440	172	157	142	128	115	101	88	76	63	51	40
1,440	1,480	180	164	149	135	121	107	93	81	69	57	45
1,480	1,520	187	171	156	141	127	114	100	87	75	63	50
1,520	1,560	194	178	163	148	134	120	106	92	80	68	56
1,560	1,600	201	186	170	154	140	126	112	99	86	74	62
1,600	1,640	208	193	177	162	147	133	119	105	91	79	67
1,640	1,680	216	200	184	169	153	139	125	111	98	85	73
1,680	1,720	224	207	192	176	160	146	132	118	104	91	78
1,720	1,760	233	214	199	183	168	152	138	124	110	96	84
1,760	1,800	242	223	206	190	175	159	144	131	117	103	90
1,800	1,840	251	232	213	198	182	166	151	137	123	109	95
1,840	1,880	259	240	221	205	189	174	158	143	130	116	102
1,880	1,920	268	249	230	212	196	181	165	150	136	122	108
1,920	1,960	277	258	239	220	204	188	172	157	142	128	115
1,960	2,000	286	267	248	229	211	195	180	164	149	135	121
2,000	2,040	295	276	256	237	218	202	187	171	156	141	127

(Continued on next page)

MARRIED Persons–MONTHLY Payroll Period
(For Wages Paid After December 1984)

And the wages are–		And the number of withholding allowances claimed is–										
At least	But less than	0	1	2	3	4	5	6	7	8	9	10
		The amount of income tax to be withheld shall be–										
$2,040	$2,080	$304	$284	$265	$246	$227	$210	$194	$178	$163	$148	$134
2,080	2,120	314	293	274	255	236	217	201	186	170	154	140
2,120	2,160	324	302	283	264	245	226	208	193	177	162	147
2,160	2,200	334	312	292	273	254	234	216	200	184	169	153
2,200	2,240	344	322	300	281	262	243	224	207	192	176	160
2,240	2,280	354	332	310	290	271	252	233	214	199	183	168
2,280	2,320	364	342	320	299	280	261	242	223	206	190	175
2,320	2,360	374	352	330	309	289	270	251	232	213	198	182
2,360	2,400	384	362	340	319	298	278	259	240	221	205	189
2,400	2,440	394	372	350	329	307	287	268	249	230	212	196
2,440	2,480	404	382	360	339	317	296	277	258	239	220	204
2,480	2,520	414	392	370	349	327	305	286	267	248	229	211
2,520	2,560	425	402	380	359	337	315	295	276	256	237	218
2,560	2,600	436	412	390	369	347	325	304	284	265	246	227
2,600	2,640	447	423	400	379	357	335	314	293	274	255	236
2,640	2,680	458	434	410	389	367	345	324	302	283	264	245
2,680	2,720	470	445	421	399	377	355	334	312	292	273	254
2,720	2,760	481	457	432	409	387	365	344	322	300	281	262
2,760	2,800	492	468	443	419	397	375	354	332	310	290	271
2,800	2,840	503	479	455	430	407	385	364	342	320	299	280
2,840	2,880	514	490	466	442	417	395	374	352	330	309	289
2,880	2,920	526	501	477	453	429	405	384	362	340	319	298
2,920	2,960	537	513	488	464	440	415	394	372	350	329	307
2,960	3,000	549	524	499	475	451	427	404	382	360	339	317
3,000	3,040	562	535	511	486	462	438	414	392	370	349	327
3,040	3,080	575	547	522	498	473	449	425	402	380	359	337
3,080	3,120	588	560	533	509	485	460	436	412	390	369	347
3,120	3,160	602	573	544	520	496	471	447	423	400	379	357
3,160	3,200	615	586	558	531	507	483	458	434	410	389	367
3,200	3,240	628	599	571	542	518	494	470	445	421	399	377
3,240	3,280	641	613	584	555	529	505	481	457	432	409	387
3,280	3,320	654	626	597	569	541	516	492	468	443	419	397
3,320	3,360	668	639	610	582	553	527	503	479	455	430	407
3,360	3,400	681	652	624	595	566	539	514	490	466	442	417
3,400	3,440	694	665	637	608	580	551	526	501	477	453	429
3,440	3,480	707	679	650	621	593	564	537	513	488	464	440
3,480	3,520	720	692	663	635	606	577	549	524	499	475	451
3,520	3,560	734	705	676	648	619	591	562	535	511	486	462
3,560	3,600	747	718	690	661	632	604	575	547	522	498	473
3,600	3,640	760	731	703	674	646	617	588	560	533	509	485
3,640	3,680	773	745	716	687	659	630	602	573	544	520	496
3,680	3,720	786	758	729	701	672	643	615	586	558	531	507
3,720	3,760	800	771	742	714	685	657	628	599	571	542	518
3,760	3,800	813	784	756	727	698	670	641	613	584	555	529
3,800	3,840	826	797	769	740	712	683	654	626	597	569	541
3,840	3,880	839	811	782	753	725	696	668	639	610	582	553
3,880	3,920	853	824	795	767	738	709	681	652	624	595	566
3,920	3,960	868	837	808	780	751	723	694	665	637	608	580
3,960	4,000	883	850	822	793	764	736	707	679	650	621	593
4,000	4,040	897	865	835	806	778	749	720	692	663	635	606
4,040	4,080	912	880	848	819	791	762	734	705	676	648	619
4,080	4,120	927	895	863	833	804	775	747	718	690	661	632
4,120	4,160	942	910	878	846	817	789	760	731	703	674	646
4,160	4,200	957	924	892	860	830	802	773	745	716	687	659
4,200	4,240	971	939	907	875	844	815	786	758	729	701	672
4,240	4,280	986	954	922	890	858	828	800	771	742	714	685
4,280	4,320	1,001	969	937	905	873	841	813	784	756	727	698
4,320	4,360	1,016	984	952	920	887	855	826	797	769	740	712
4,360	4,400	1,031	998	966	934	902	870	839	811	782	753	725
4,400	4,440	1,045	1,013	981	949	917	885	853	824	795	767	738
4,440	4,480	1,060	1,028	996	964	932	900	868	837	808	780	751
4,480	4,520	1,075	1,043	1,011	979	947	915	883	850	822	793	764
4,520	4,560	1,090	1,058	1,026	994	961	929	897	865	835	806	778
4,560	4,600	1,105	1,072	1,040	1,008	976	944	912	880	848	819	791
4,600	4,640	1,119	1,087	1,055	1,023	991	959	927	895	863	833	804
4,640	4,680	1,134	1,102	1,070	1,038	1,006	974	942	910	878	846	817
4,680	4,720	1,149	1,117	1,085	1,053	1,021	989	957	924	892	860	830
4,720	4,760	1,164	1,132	1,100	1,068	1,035	1,003	971	939	907	875	844
4,760	4,800	1,179	1,146	1,114	1,082	1,050	1,018	986	954	922	890	858
		37 percent of the excess over $4,800 plus–										
$4,800 and over		1,186	1,154	1,122	1,090	1,058	1,026	994	961	929	897	865

SINGLE Persons–DAILY OR MISCELLANEOUS Payroll Period

(For Wages Paid After December 1984)

And the wages are–		And the number of withholding allowances claimed is–										
At least	But less than	0	1	2	3	4	5	6	7	8	9	10
		The amount of income tax to be withheld shall be–										
$0	$10	$0	$0	$0	$0	$0	$0	$0	$0	$0	$0	$0
10	12	1	0	0	0	0	0	0	0	0	0	0
12	14	1	0	0	0	0	0	0	0	0	0	0
14	16	1	1	0	0	0	0	0	0	0	0	0
16	18	1	1	0	0	0	0	0	0	0	0	0
18	20	2	1	1	0	0	0	0	0	0	0	0
20	22	2	1	1	0	0	0	0	0	0	0	0
22	24	2	2	1	1	0	0	0	0	0	0	0
24	26	3	2	1	1	0	0	0	0	0	0	0
26	28	3	2	2	1	1	0	0	0	0	0	0
28	30	3	3	2	1	1	0	0	0	0	0	0
30	32	4	3	2	2	1	1	0	0	0	0	0
32	34	4	3	3	2	1	1	0	0	0	0	0
34	36	4	4	3	2	2	1	0	0	0	0	0
36	38	4	4	3	3	2	1	1	0	0	0	0
38	40	5	4	4	3	2	2	1	1	0	0	0
40	42	5	4	4	3	3	2	2	1	1	0	0
42	44	5	5	4	4	3	3	2	1	1	0	0
44	46	6	5	4	4	4	3	2	2	1	1	0
46	48	6	5	5	4	4	3	3	2	1	1	0
48	50	7	6	5	4	4	3	3	2	1	1	0
50	52	7	6	5	5	4	4	3	2	1	1	1
52	54	7	7	6	5	4	4	3	3	2	1	1
54	56	8	7	6	5	5	4	4	3	2	1	1
56	58	8	7	7	6	5	5	4	4	3	2	1
58	60	9	8	7	6	5	5	4	4	3	2	2
60	62	9	8	7	7	6	5	5	4	4	3	2
62	64	10	9	8	7	7	6	5	5	4	3	2
64	66	10	9	9	8	7	7	6	5	4	4	3
66	68	11	10	9	8	8	7	6	5	5	4	3
68	70	11	10	9	8	7	7	6	5	4	4	3
70	72	12	11	10	9	8	7	7	6	5	4	4
72	74	12	11	10	9	8	8	7	7	6	5	4
74	76	13	12	11	10	9	8	7	7	6	5	5
76	78	13	12	11	10	9	9	8	7	7	6	5
78	80	14	13	12	11	10	9	8	7	6	5	5
80	82	14	13	13	12	11	10	9	8	7	6	5
82	84	15	14	13	12	11	10	9	8	7	6	5
84	86	15	14	13	13	12	11	9	8	7	6	6
86	88	16	15	14	13	12	11	10	9	8	7	6
88	90	16	15	14	13	12	11	10	9	8	7	7
90	92	17	16	15	14	13	12	11	10	9	8	7
92	94	17	16	15	15	13	12	11	10	9	8	7
94	96	18	17	16	16	14	13	12	11	10	9	8
96	98	19	17	16	16	15	14	13	12	11	10	9
98	100	19	18	17	16	15	14	13	12	11	10	9
100	102	20	19	18	17	16	15	14	13	12	11	9
102	104	20	19	18	17	16	15	14	13	12	11	10
104	106	21	20	19	18	17	16	15	14	13	12	11
106	108	22	20	19	18	17	16	15	14	13	12	11
108	110	22	21	20	19	17	16	15	14	13	12	11
110	112	23	22	20	19	18	17	16	15	14	13	12
112	114	23	22	21	20	19	18	17	16	15	14	12
114	116	24	23	22	21	20	19	18	17	16	15	13
116	118	25	23	22	22	21	20	19	17	16	15	13
118	120	25	24	23	22	20	19	18	17	16	15	14
120	122	26	25	24	23	22	20	19	18	17	16	14
122	124	27	25	25	24	23	22	20	19	18	17	15
124	126	28	26	26	25	23	22	21	20	19	18	15
126	128	28	27	27	25	24	23	22	20	19	18	16
128	130	29	28	26	25	23	22	21	20	19	17	16
130	132	30	28	27	25	24	23	22	21	20	19	17
132	134	30	29	28	26	25	23	23	22	21	20	17
134	136	31	30	28	27	25	24	23	22	22	20	18
136	138	32	30	29	28	26	25	24	23	22	21	19
138	140	32	31	30	28	27	25	24	23	22	20	19
140	142	33	32	30	29	28	26	25	24	23	21	20
142	144	34	32	31	30	28	27	25	24	23	22	20
144	146	35	33	32	31	30	28	26	25	24	23	21
146	148	35	34	32	32	31	30	28	27	25	23	22

(Continued on next page)

SINGLE Persons—DAILY OR MISCELLANEOUS Payroll Period
(For Wages Paid After December 1984)

And the wages are—		And the number of withholding allowances claimed is—										
At least	But less than	0	1	2	3	4	5	6	7	8	9	10
		The amount of income tax to be withheld shall be—										
$148	$150	$36	$35	$33	$32	$30	$29	$28	$26	$25	$23	$22
150	152	37	35	34	32	31	30	28	27	25	24	23
152	154	38	36	35	33	32	30	29	28	26	25	23
154	156	38	37	35	34	32	31	30	28	27	25	24
156	158	39	38	36	35	33	32	30	29	28	26	25
158	160	40	38	37	35	34	32	31	30	28	27	25
160	162	41	39	38	36	35	33	32	30	29	28	26
162	164	41	40	38	37	35	34	32	31	30	28	27
164	166	42	41	39	38	36	35	33	32	30	29	28
166	168	43	41	40	38	37	35	34	32	31	30	28
168	170	44	42	41	39	38	36	35	33	32	30	29
170	172	44	43	41	40	38	37	35	34	32	31	30
172	174	45	44	42	41	39	38	36	35	33	32	30
174	176	46	44	43	41	40	38	37	35	34	32	31
176	178	47	45	44	42	41	39	38	36	35	33	32
178	180	47	46	44	43	41	40	38	37	35	34	32
180	182	48	47	45	44	42	41	39	38	36	35	33
182	184	49	47	46	44	43	41	40	38	37	35	34
184	186	49	48	47	45	44	42	41	39	38	36	35
186	188	50	49	47	46	44	43	41	40	38	37	35
188	190	51	49	48	47	45	44	42	41	39	38	36
190	192	52	50	49	47	46	44	43	41	40	38	37
192	194	52	51	49	48	47	45	44	42	41	39	38
194	196	53	52	50	49	47	46	44	43	41	40	38
196	198	54	52	51	49	48	47	45	44	42	41	39
198	200	55	53	52	50	49	47	46	44	43	41	40
200	202	55	54	52	51	49	48	47	45	44	42	41
202	204	56	55	53	52	50	49	47	46	44	43	41
204	206	57	55	54	52	51	49	48	47	45	44	42
206	208	58	56	55	53	52	50	49	47	46	44	43
208	210	58	57	55	54	52	51	49	48	47	45	44
210	212	59	58	56	55	53	52	50	49	47	46	44
212	214	60	58	57	55	54	52	51	49	48	47	45
214	216	61	59	58	56	55	53	52	50	49	47	46
216	218	61	60	58	57	55	54	52	51	49	48	47
218	220	62	61	59	58	56	55	53	52	50	49	47
220	222	63	61	60	58	57	55	54	52	51	49	48
222	224	64	62	61	59	58	56	55	53	52	50	49
224	226	64	63	61	60	58	57	55	54	52	51	49
226	228	65	64	62	61	59	58	56	55	53	52	50
228	230	66	64	63	61	60	58	57	55	54	52	51
230	232	66	65	64	62	61	59	58	56	55	53	52
232	234	67	66	64	63	61	60	58	57	55	54	52
234	236	68	66	65	64	62	61	59	58	56	55	53
236	238	69	67	66	64	63	61	60	58	57	55	54
238	240	69	68	66	65	64	62	61	59	58	56	55
240	242	70	69	67	66	64	63	61	60	58	57	55
242	244	71	69	68	66	65	64	62	61	59	58	56
244	246	72	70	69	67	66	64	63	61	60	58	57
246	248	72	71	69	68	66	65	64	62	61	59	58
248	250	73	72	70	69	67	66	64	63	61	60	58
250	252	74	72	71	69	68	66	65	64	62	61	59
252	254	75	73	72	70	69	67	66	64	63	61	60
254	256	75	74	72	71	69	68	66	65	64	62	61
256	258	76	75	73	72	70	69	67	66	64	63	61
258	260	77	75	74	72	71	69	68	66	65	64	62
260	262	78	76	75	73	72	70	69	67	66	64	63
262	264	78	77	75	74	72	71	69	68	66	65	64
264	266	79	78	76	75	73	72	70	69	67	66	64
266	268	80	78	77	75	74	72	71	69	68	66	65
268	270	81	79	78	76	75	73	72	70	69	67	66
270	272	81	80	78	77	75	74	72	71	69	68	66
272	274	82	81	79	78	76	75	73	72	70	69	67
274	276	83	81	80	78	77	75	74	72	71	69	68
276	278	84	82	81	79	78	76	75	73	72	70	69
278	280	84	83	81	80	78	77	75	74	72	71	69
		37 percent of the excess over $280 plus—										
$280 and over		85	83	82	80	79	77	76	74	73	71	70

MARRIED Persons–DAILY OR MISCELLANEOUS Payroll Period
(For Wages Paid After December 1984)

And the wages are–		And the number of withholding allowances claimed is–										
At least	But less than	0	1	2	3	4	5	6	7	8	9	10
		The amount of income tax to be withheld shall be–										
$0	$14	$0	$0	$0	$0	$0	$0	$0	$0	$0	$0	$0
14	16	1	0	0	0	0	0	0	0	0	0	0
16	18	1	0	0	0	0	0	0	0	0	0	0
18	20	1	1	0	0	0	0	0	0	0	0	0
20	22	1	1	0	0	0	0	0	0	0	0	0
22	24	2	1	1	0	0	0	0	0	0	0	0
24	26	2	1	1	0	0	0	0	0	0	0	0
26	28	2	2	1	1	0	0	0	0	0	0	0
28	30	2	2	1	1	0	0	0	0	0	0	0
30	32	3	2	2	2	1	0	0	0	0	0	0
32	34	3	2	2	1	1	0	0	0	0	0	0
34	36	3	3	2	2	1	1	0	0	0	0	0
36	38	3	3	2	2	1	1	0	0	0	0	0
38	40	4	3	3	2	2	1	0	0	0	0	0
40	42	4	3	3	3	2	1	1	0	0	0	0
42	44	4	4	3	3	2	2	1	1	0	0	0
44	46	5	4	3	3	2	2	1	1	0	0	0
46	48	5	4	4	3	3	2	2	1	1	0	0
48	50	5	5	4	3	3	2	2	1	1	0	0
50	52	6	5	4	4	3	3	2	2	1	1	1
52	54	6	5	5	4	3	3	2	2	1	1	0
54	56	6	6	5	5	4	3	3	2	2	1	1
56	58	6	6	5	5	4	4	3	2	2	1	1
58	60	7	6	6	5	4	4	3	3	2	2	1
60	62	7	7	6	6	5	4	4	3	3	2	1
62	64	8	7	6	6	5	4	4	3	3	2	2
64	66	8	7	6	6	5	5	4	4	3	3	2
66	68	8	8	7	6	6	5	4	4	3	3	2
68	70	9	8	7	7	6	5	5	4	3	3	2
70	72	9	8	8	7	6	6	5	4	4	3	3
72	74	9	9	8	7	6	6	6	5	4	3	3
74	76	10	9	8	8	7	6	6	5	4	4	3
76	78	10	9	9	8	7	6	6	5	5	4	3
78	80	10	10	9	9	8	7	6	6	5	4	4
80	82	11	10	10	9	8	8	7	6	6	5	4
82	84	11	10	10	9	8	8	7	6	6	5	4
84	86	12	11	11	9	9	8	7	6	6	5	5
86	88	12	11	10	10	9	8	8	7	6	6	5
88	90	13	12	11	11	10	9	8	7	6	6	5
90	92	13	12	12	11	10	9	9	8	7	6	6
92	94	14	13	12	11	10	9	9	8	7	6	6
94	96	14	13	12	11	10	10	9	8	7	6	6
96	98	15	14	13	12	11	10	9	9	8	7	6
98	100	15	14	13	12	11	10	10	9	8	7	6
100	102	16	15	14	13	12	11	10	9	9	8	7
102	104	16	15	14	13	12	11	10	10	9	8	8
104	106	17	16	15	14	13	12	11	10	10	9	8
106	108	17	16	15	14	13	12	11	11	10	9	8
108	110	18	17	16	15	14	13	12	11	10	10	9
110	112	18	17	16	15	14	13	12	12	11	10	9
112	114	19	18	17	16	15	14	13	12	11	10	9
114	116	19	18	17	16	15	14	13	12	11	10	10
116	118	20	19	18	17	16	15	14	13	12	11	10
118	120	20	19	18	17	16	15	14	13	12	11	10
120	122	21	20	19	18	17	16	15	14	13	12	11
122	124	21	20	19	18	17	16	15	14	13	12	11
124	126	22	21	20	19	18	17	16	15	14	13	12
126	128	22	21	20	19	18	17	16	15	14	13	12
128	130	23	22	21	20	19	18	17	16	15	14	13
130	132	23	22	21	20	19	18	17	16	15	14	13
132	134	24	23	22	21	20	19	18	17	16	15	14
134	136	25	23	22	21	20	19	18	17	16	15	14
136	138	25	24	23	22	21	20	19	18	17	16	15
138	140	26	25	23	22	21	20	19	18	17	16	15
140	142	26	25	24	23	22	21	20	19	18	17	16
142	144	27	26	25	23	22	21	20	19	18	17	16
144	146	28	26	25	24	23	22	21	20	19	18	17
146	148	28	27	26	25	23	22	21	20	19	18	17
148	150	29	28	27	25	24	23	22	21	20	19	18
150	152	30	28	28	26	25	23	22	22	21	20	19

(Continued on next page)

MARRIED Persons–DAILY OR MISCELLANEOUS Payroll Period
(For Wages Paid After December 1984)

And the wages are–		And the number of withholding allowances claimed is–										
At least	But less than	0	1	2	3	4	5	6	7	8	9	10
		The amount of income tax to be withheld shall be–										
$152	$154	$30	$29	$28	$26	$25	$24	$23	$22	$21	$20	$19
154	156	31	30	28	27	26	25	23	22	21	20	19
156	158	32	30	29	28	26	25	24	23	22	21	20
158	160	32	31	30	28	27	26	25	23	22	21	20
160	162	33	32	30	29	28	26	25	24	23	22	21
162	164	34	32	31	30	28	27	26	25	23	22	21
164	166	34	33	32	30	29	28	26	25	24	23	22
166	168	35	34	32	31	30	28	27	26	25	23	22
168	170	36	34	33	32	30	29	28	26	25	24	23
170	172	36	35	34	32	31	30	28	27	26	25	23
172	174	37	36	34	33	32	30	29	28	26	25	24
174	176	38	36	35	34	32	31	30	28	27	26	25
176	178	38	37	36	34	33	32	30	29	28	26	25
178	180	39	38	36	35	34	32	31	30	28	27	26
180	182	40	38	38	37	36	33	32	30	30	29	26
182	184	40	39	38	36	35	34	32	31	30	28	27
184	186	41	40	38	37	36	34	33	32	30	29	28
186	188	42	40	39	38	36	35	34	32	31	30	28
188	190	43	41	40	38	37	36	34	33	32	30	29
190	192	43	42	40	39	38	36	35	34	32	31	30
192	194	44	43	41	40	38	37	36	34	33	32	30
194	196	45	43	42	40	39	38	36	35	34	32	31
196	198	46	44	43	41	40	38	37	36	35	33	32
198	200	46	45	43	42	40	39	38	36	35	34	32
200	202	47	46	44	43	41	40	38	37	36	34	33
202	204	48	46	45	43	42	40	39	38	36	35	34
204	206	49	47	46	44	43	41	40	38	37	36	34
206	208	49	48	46	45	43	42	40	39	38	36	35
208	210	50	49	47	46	44	43	41	40	38	37	36
210	212	51	49	48	46	45	43	42	40	39	38	36
212	214	52	50	49	47	46	44	43	41	40	38	37
214	216	52	51	49	48	46	45	43	42	40	39	38
216	218	53	52	50	49	47	46	44	43	41	40	38
218	220	54	52	51	49	48	46	45	43	42	40	39
220	222	55	53	52	50	49	47	46	44	43	41	40
222	224	55	54	52	51	49	48	46	45	43	42	40
224	226	56	55	53	52	50	49	47	46	44	43	41
226	228	57	55	54	52	51	49	48	46	45	43	42
228	230	57	56	55	53	52	50	49	47	46	44	43
230	232	58	57	55	54	52	51	49	48	46	45	43
232	234	59	57	56	55	53	52	50	49	47	46	44
234	236	60	58	57	55	54	52	51	49	48	46	45
236	238	60	59	57	56	55	53	52	50	49	47	46
238	240	61	60	58	57	55	54	52	51	49	48	46
240	242	62	60	59	57	56	55	53	52	50	49	47
242	244	63	61	60	58	57	55	54	52	51	49	48
244	246	63	62	60	59	57	56	55	53	52	50	49
246	248	64	63	61	60	58	57	55	54	52	51	49
248	250	65	63	62	60	59	57	56	55	53	52	50
250	252	66	64	63	61	60	58	57	55	54	52	51
252	254	66	65	63	62	60	59	57	56	55	53	52
254	256	67	66	64	63	61	60	58	57	55	54	52
256	258	68	66	65	63	62	60	59	57	56	55	53
258	260	69	67	66	64	63	61	60	58	57	55	54
260	262	69	68	66	65	63	62	60	59	57	56	55
262	264	70	69	67	66	64	63	61	60	58	57	55
264	266	71	69	68	66	65	63	62	60	59	57	56
266	268	72	70	69	67	66	64	63	61	60	58	57
268	270	72	71	69	68	66	65	63	62	60	59	57
270	272	* 73	72	70	69	67	66	64	63	61	60	58
272	274	74	72	71	69	68	66	65	63	62	60	59
274	276	75	73	72	70	69	67	66	64	63	61	60
276	278	75	74	72	71	69	68	66	65	63	62	60
278	280	76	75	73	72	70	69	67	66	64	63	61
280	282	77	75	74	72	71	69	68	66	65	63	62
282	284	77	76	75	73	72	70	69	67	66	64	63
		37 percent of the excess over $284 plus–										
$284 and over		78	76	75	73	72	70	69	67	66	65	63

COMPUTING YOUR INCOME TAX WITHHOLDING USING THE PERCENTAGE METHOD

There are several different computational techniques and tables for using the percentage method. Circular E, "Employer's Tax Guide," shows the following example of the regular percentage method.

Income Tax Withholding— Percentage Method

If you do not want to use the wage bracket tables to figure how much income tax to withhold, you can use a percentage computation based on the table below and the appropriate rate table. This method works for any number of withholding allowances the employee claims.

Percentage Method Income Tax Withholding Table

Payroll Period	One withholding allowance
Weekly	$20.00
Biweekly	40.00
Semimonthly	43.33
Monthly	86.67
Quarterly	260.00
Semiannually	520.00
Annually	1,040.00
Daily or miscellaneous (each day of the payroll period)	4.00

Use these steps to figure the income tax to withhold under the percentage method:

(a) Multiply one withholding allowance (see table above) by the number of allowances the employee claims.

(b) Subtract that amount from the employee's wages.

(c) Determine amount to withhold from appropriate table.

Example—An unmarried employee is paid $150 weekly. This employee has in effect a Form W-4 claiming one personal allowance and the special withholding allowance. Using the percentage method, figure the income tax as follows:

(1) Total wage payment	$150.00
(2) One allowance	$20.00
(3) Allowances claimed on Form W-4 (including the special withholding allowance)	2
(4) Line 2 times line 3	40.00
(5) Amount subject to withholding (subtract line 4 from line 1)	$110.00
(6) Tax to be withheld on $110.00 from Table 1—single person: tax on first $84.00	6.84
Tax on remainder $26.00 @ 15%	3.90
Total to be withheld	$ 10.74

To figure the income tax to withhold, you may reduce the last digit of the wages to zero, or figure the wages to the nearest dollar.

Tables for Percentage Method of Withholding
(For Wages Paid After December 1984)

TABLE 1—If the Payroll Period With Respect to an Employee is Weekly

(a) SINGLE person—including head of household:

If the amount of wages is:		The amount of income tax to be withheld shall be:	of excess over—
Not over $27 0			
Over—	But not over—		
$27	—$84	.12%	—$27
$84	—$185 . . .	.$6.84 plus 15%	—$84
$185	—$292 . . .	.$21.99 plus 19%	—$185
$292	—$440 . . .	.$42.32 plus 25%	—$292
$440	—$556 . . .	.$79.32 plus 30%	—$440
$556	—$663 . . .	.$114.12 plus 34%	—$556
$663	. . . .	.$150.50 plus 37%	—$663

(b) MARRIED person—

If the amount of wages is:		The amount of income tax to be withheld shall be:	of excess over—
Not over $48 0			
Over—	But not over—		
$48	—$192 . .	.12%	—$48
$192	—$384 . .	.$17.28 plus 17%	—$192
$384	—$472 . .	.$49.92 plus 22%	—$384
$472	—$578 . .	.$69.28 plus 25%	—$472
$578	—$684 . .	.$95.78 plus 28%	—$578
$684	—$897 . .	.$125.46 plus 33%	—$684
$897	. . . . . .	.$195.75 plus 37%	—$897

The problem with the regular percentage method is that several unnecessary mathematical steps must be used to compute the amount of withholding. Therefore, the IRS has designed additional tables for the percentage method that make the mathematics simpler and the computations easy to do with a pocket calculator without having to use a memory feature, or without having to do additional math on the side.

The next table you should become familiar with is the one below:

(For Wages Paid After December 1984)

Wage Bracket Percentage Method Table for Computing
Income Tax Withholding from Gross Wages

Monthly Payroll Period

	Single Persons					Married Persons			
If the number of allowances is–	And gross wages are–		Subtract from gross wages[1]	Multiply remainder by–	If the number of allowances is–	And gross wages are–		Subtract from gross wages[1]	Multiply remainder by–
	Over	But not over				Over	But not over		
0	$0	$364.00	$118.00	12%	0	$0	$833.00	$208.00	12%
	364.00	800.00	167.20	15%		833.00	1,663.00	391.82	17%
	800.00	1,267.00	300.42	19%		1,663.00	2,047.00	680.73	22%
	1,267.00	1,908.00	532.40	25%		2,047.00	2,507.00	844.68	25%
	1,908.00	2,411.00	761.67	30%		2,507.00	2,966.00	1,022.79	28%
	2,411.00	2,871.00	955.71	34%		2,966.00	3,885.00	1,317.21	33%
	2,871.00	....	1,111.00	37%		3,885.00	....	1,594.81	37%
1	$0	$450.67	$204.67	12%	1	$0	$919.67	$294.67	12%
	450.67	886.67	253.87	15%		919.67	1,749.67	478.49	17%
	886.67	1,353.67	387.09	19%		1,749.67	2,133.67	767.40	22%
	1,353.67	1,994.67	619.07	25%		2,133.67	2,593.67	931.35	25%
	1,994.67	2,497.67	848.34	30%		2,593.67	3,052.67	1,109.46	28%
	2,497.67	2,957.67	1,042.38	34%		3,052.67	3,971.67	1,403.88	33%
	2,957.67	....	1,197.67	37%		3,971.67	....	1,681.48	37%
2	$0	$537.34	$291.34	12%	2	$0	$1,006.34	$381.34	12%
	537.34	973.34	340.54	15%		1,006.34	1,836.34	565.16	17%
	973.34	1,440.34	473.76	19%		1,836.34	2,220.34	854.07	22%
	1,440.34	2,081.34	705.74	25%		2,220.34	2,680.34	1,018.02	25%
	2,081.34	2,584.34	935.01	30%		2,680.34	3,139.34	1,196.13	28%
	2,584.34	3,044.34	1,129.05	34%		3,139.34	4,058.34	1,490.55	33%
	3,044.34	....	1,284.34	37%		4,058.34	....	1,768.15	37%

This table is easy to use because it is designed with the withholding allowance exemption amounts already built in. All you need to know are your gross wages and the number of allowances you are entitled to claim. Just follow the instructions across and you will quickly find the amount to be withheld.

Example 1

Danny is married, claims two allowances, and earned $2,876 this month. His withholding is computed as follows:

Gross wages $2,876.00
Subtract table factor .... − 1,196.13
Equals $1,679.87
Multiply by table factor .... × ___28%
Amount to be withheld = $ 470.36

The only disadvantage to this table is that it only goes up to nine withholding allowances. The instructions tell you how to adapt the tables for allowances in excess of nine, but at that point the mathematics become a little more complicated, and there is an easier table to use. Those claiming more than nine withholding allowances should use the following table:

(For Wages Paid After December 1984)

Alternative 1.—Tables for Percentage Method Withholding Computations

Table A(1)—WEEKLY PAYROLL PERIOD (Amount for each allowance claimed $20.00)

Single Person				Married Person			
If the wage in excess of allowance amount is:		The income tax to be withheld shall be:		If the wage in excess of allowance amount is:		The income tax to be withheld shall be:	
Over—	But not over—	Of such wage—	From product	Over—	But not over—	Of such wage—	From product
$0	—$27	0		$0	—$48	0	
$27	—$84	12% less $3.24		$48	—$192	12% less $5.76	
$84	—$185	15% less $5.76		$192	—$384	17% less $15.36	
$185	—$292	19% less $13.16		$384	—$472	22% less $34.56	
$292	—$440	25% less $30.68		$472	—$578	25% less $48.72	
$440	—$556	30% less $52.68		$578	—$684	28% less $66.06	
$556	—$663	34% less $74.92		$684	—$897	33% less $100.26	
$663	—	37% less $94.81		$897	—	37% less $136.14	

In conjunction with this excerpt from the table (computed to 25 allowances) on page 136:

Withholding Allowances	1	2	3	4
Weekly	20.00	40.00	60.00	80.00
Biweekly	40.00	80.00	120.00	160.00
Semimonthly	43.33	86.66	129.99	173.32
Monthly	86.67	173.34	260.01	346.68
Quarterly	260.00	520.00	780.00	1,040.00
Semiannually	520.00	1,040.00	1,560.00	2,080.00
Annually	1,040.00	2,080.00	3,120.00	4,160.00

The difference between the Alternative 1 Percentage Method Table and the Wage Bracket Percentage Method Table shown on page 133 is the extra math step required in the Alternative 1 Table.

To use the Alternative 1 Table you must first find the withholding exemption allowance amount by referring to the *Percentage Method Allowance Amounts Table* on page 136. (To use that table all you need to know is your payroll period and the number of withholding allowances you are entitled to claim.)

The next step is to subtract the applicable amount of exempt income (or allowance amount) found in the *Percentage Method Allowance Amounts Table* (page 136) from your gross wages for the pay period. The difference is referred to as "the wage in excess of the allowance amount." To find the amount to be withheld, you go to the appropriate Alternative 1 Percentage Method Table and follow the calculation steps given there.

Example 2

Bob is single, has a very high income, and is entitled to eleven withholding allowances due to excess itemized deductions, alimony payments, employee business expenses, and a net operating loss carry-over from previous years. For the current week he earned $1,500. His withholding is computed using the following steps:

Amount of gross wages $1,500.00
Subtract the appropriate allowance amount from the
    Percentage Method Allowance Amount Table (go to
    eleven allowances and down to the weekly column)   −220.00

Wage in excess of allowance amount $1,280.00
Multiply by table factor .... ×   37%

Equals .... $ 473.60
Subtract table factor .... −   94.81

Amount to be withheld .... $ 378.79

PERCENTAGE METHOD ALLOWANCE AMOUNTS COMPUTED FOR INCOME TAX WITHHOLDING TABLES

Withholding Allowances	1	2	3	4	5	6	7	8	9	10	11	12	13
Weekly	20.00	40.00	60.00	80.00	100.00	120.00	140.00	160.00	180.00	200.00	220.00	240.00	260.00
Biweekly	40.00	80.00	120.00	160.00	200.00	240.00	280.00	320.00	360.00	400.00	440.00	480.00	520.00
Semimonthly	43.33	86.66	129.99	173.32	216.65	259.98	303.31	346.64	389.97	433.30	476.63	519.96	563.29
Monthly	86.67	173.34	260.01	346.68	433.35	520.02	606.69	693.36	780.03	866.70	953.37	1,040.04	1,126.71
Quarterly	260.00	520.00	780.00	1,040.00	1,300.00	1,560.00	1,820.00	2,080.00	2,340.00	2,600.00	2,860.00	3,120.00	3,380.00
Semiannually	520.00	1,040.00	1,560.00	2,080.00	2,600.00	3,120.00	3,640.00	4,160.00	4,680.00	5,200.00	5,720.00	6,240.00	6,760.00
Annually	1,040.00	2,080.00	3,120.00	4,160.00	5,200.00	6,240.00	7,280.00	8,320.00	9,360.00	10,400.00	11,440.00	12,480.00	13,520.00
Daily or Miscellaneous	4.00	8.00	12.00	16.00	20.00	24.00	28.00	32.00	36.00	40.00	44.00	48.00	52.00

Withholding Allowances	14	15	16	17	18	19	20	21	22	23	24	25
Weekly	280.00	300.00	320.00	340.00	360.00	380.00	400.00	420.00	440.00	460.00	480.00	500.00
Biweekly	560.00	600.00	640.00	680.00	720.00	760.00	800.00	840.00	880.00	920.00	960.00	1,000.00
Semimonthly	606.62	649.95	693.28	736.61	779.94	823.27	866.60	909.93	953.26	996.59	1,039.92	1,083.25
Monthly	1,213.38	1,300.05	1,386.72	1,473.39	1,560.06	1,646.73	1,733.40	1,820.07	1,906.74	1,993.41	2,080.08	2,166.75
Quarterly	3,640.00	3,900.00	4,160.00	4,420.00	4,680.00	4,940.00	5,200.00	5,460.00	5,720.00	5,980.00	6,240.00	6,500.00
Semiannually	7,280.00	7,800.00	8,320.00	8,840.00	9,360.00	9,880.00	10,400.00	10,920.00	11,440.00	11,960.00	12,480.00	13,000.00
Annually	14,560.00	15,600.00	16,640.00	17,680.00	18,720.00	19,760.00	20,800.00	21,840.00	22,880.00	23,920.00	24,960.00	26,000.00
Daily or Miscellaneous	56.00	60.00	64.00	68.00	72.00	76.00	80.00	84.00	88.00	92.00	96.00	100.00

(For Wages Paid After December 1984)

Alternative 1.—Tables for Percentage Method Withholding Computations

Table A(1)—WEEKLY PAYROLL PERIOD (Amount for each allowance claimed $20.00)

Single Person				Married Person			
If the wage in excess of allowance amount is:		The income tax to be withheld shall be:		If the wage in excess of allowance amount is:		The income tax to be withheld shall be:	
Over—	But not over—	Of such wage—	From product	Over—	But not over—	Of such wage—	From product
$0	—$27		0	$0	—$48		0
$27	—$84	12% less	$3.24	$48	—$192	12% less	$5.76
$84	—$185	15% less	$5.76	$192	—$384	17% less	$15.36
$185	—$292	19% less	$13.16	$384	—$472	22% less	$34.56
$292	—$440	25% less	$30.68	$472	—$578	25% less	$48.72
$440	—$556	30% less	$52.68	$578	—$684	28% less	$66.06
$556	—$663	34% less	$74.92	$684	—$897	33% less	$100.26
$663	—	37% less	$94.81	$897	—	37% less	$136.14

Table B(1)—BIWEEKLY PAYROLL PERIOD (Amount for each allowance claimed $40.00)

Single Person				Married Person			
If the wage in excess of allowance amount is:		The income tax to be withheld shall be:		If the wage in excess of allowance amount is:		The income tax to be withheld shall be:	
Over—	But not over—	Of such wage—	From product	Over—	But not over—	Of such wage—	From product
$0	—$55		0	$0	—$96		0
$55	—$168	12% less	$6.60	$96	—$385	12% less	$11.52
$168	—$369	15% less	$11.64	$385	—$767	17% less	$30.77
$369	—$585	19% less	$26.40	$767	—$945	22% less	$69.12
$585	—$881	25% less	$61.50	$945	—$1,157	25% less	$97.47
$881	—$1,113	30% less	$105.55	$1,157	—$1,369	28% less	$132.18
$1,113	—$1,325	34% less	$150.07	$1,369	—$1,793	33% less	$200.63
$1,325	—	37% less	$189.82	$1,793	—	37% less	$272.35

Table C(1)—SEMIMONTHLY PAYROLL PERIOD (Amount for each allowance claimed $43.33)

Single Person				Married Person			
If the wage in excess of allowance amount is:		The income tax to be withheld shall be:		If the wage in excess of allowance amount is:		The income tax to be withheld shall be:	
Over—	But not over—	Of such wage—	From product	Over—	But not over—	Of such wage—	From product
$0	—$59		0	$0	—$104		0
$59	—$182	12% less	$7.08	$104	—$417	12% less	$12.48
$182	—$400	15% less	$12.54	$417	—$831	17% less	$33.33
$400	—$633	19% less	$28.54	$831	—$1,023	22% less	$74.88
$633	—$954	25% less	$66.52	$1,023	—$1,253	25% less	$105.57
$954	—$1,205	30% less	$114.22	$1,253	—$1,483	28% less	$143.16
$1,205	—$1,435	34% less	$162.42	$1,483	—$1,943	33% less	$217.31
$1,435	—	37% less	$205.47	$1,943	—	37% less	$295.03

Table D(1)—MONTHLY PAYROLL PERIOD (Amount for each allowance claimed $86.67)

Single Person				Married Person			
If the wage in excess of allowance amount is:		The income tax to be withheld shall be:		If the wage in excess of allowance amount is:		The income tax to be withheld shall be:	
Over—	But not over—	Of such wage—	From product	Over—	But not over—	Of such wage—	From product
$0	—$118		0	$0	—$208		0
$118	—$364	12% less	$14.16	$208	—$833	12% less	$24.96
$364	—$800	15% less	$25.08	$833	—$1,663	17% less	$66.61
$800	—$1,267	19% less	$57.08	$1,663	—$2,047	22% less	$149.76
$1,267	—$1,908	25% less	$133.10	$2,047	—$2,507	25% less	$211.17
$1,908	—$2,411	30% less	$228.50	$2,507	—$2,966	28% less	$286.38
$2,411	—$2,871	34% less	$324.94	$2,966	—$3,885	33% less	$434.68
$2,871	—	37% less	$411.07	$3,885	—	37% less	$590.08

Table E(1)—DAILY OR MISCELLANEOUS PAYROLL PERIOD (Amount for each allowance claimed per day for such period—$4.00)

Single Person				Married Person			
If wage in excess of allowance amount divided by the number of days in the pay period is:		The income tax to be withheld multiplied by the number of days in such period shall be:		If wage in excess of allowance amount divided by the number of days in the pay period is:		The income tax to be withheld multiplied by the number of days in such period shall be:	
Over—	But not over—	Of such wage—	From product	Over—	But not over—	Of such wage—	From product
$0.00	—$5.50		0	$0.00	—$9.60		0
$5.50	—$16.80	12% less	$0.66	$9.60	—$38.50	12% less	$1.15
$16.80	—$36.90	15% less	$1.16	$38.50	—$76.70	17% less	$3.08
$36.90	—$58.50	19% less	$2.64	$76.70	—$94.50	22% less	$6.91
$58.50	—$88.10	25% less	$6.15	$94.50	—$115.70	25% less	$9.75
$88.10	—$111.30	30% less	$10.56	$115.70	—$136.90	28% less	$13.22
$111.30	—$132.50	34% less	$15.01	$136.90	—$179.30	33% less	$20.06
$132.50	—	37% less	$18.98	$179.30	—	37% less	$27.24

Note.—The adjustment factors may be reduced by one-half cent (e.g., 3.24 to 3.235; 5.76 to 5.755) to eliminate separate half rounding operations.

The first two brackets of these tables may be combined, provided zero withholding is used to credit withholding amounts computed by the combined bracket rates, e.g., $0 to $27 and $27 to $84 combined to read, Over $0, But not over $84.

The employee's excess wage (gross wage less amount for allowances claimed) is used with the applicable percentage rates and subtraction factors to calculate the amount of income tax withheld.

(For Wages Paid After December 1984)

Wage Bracket Percentage Method Table for Computing
Income Tax Withholding from Gross Wages

Weekly Payroll Period

	Single Persons					Married Persons			
If the number of allowances is—	And gross wages are—		Subtract from gross wages[1]	Multiply remainder by—	If the number of allowances is—	And gross wages are—		Subtract from gross wages[1]	Multiply remainder by—
	Over	But not over				Over	But not over		
0	$0	$84.00	$27.00	12%	**0**	$0	$192.00	$48.00	12%
	84.00	185.00	38.40	15%		192.00	384.00	90.35	17%
	185.00	292.00	69.26	19%		384.00	472.00	157.09	22%
	292.00	440.00	122.72	25%		472.00	578.00	194.88	25%
	440.00	556.00	175.60	30%		578.00	684.00	235.93	28%
	556.00	663.00	220.35	34%		684.00	897.00	303.82	33%
	663.00	....	256.24	37%		897.00	....	367.95	37%
1	$0	$104.00	$47.00	12%	**1**	$0	$212.00	$68.00	12%
	104.00	205.00	58.40	15%		212.00	404.00	110.35	17%
	205.00	312.00	89.26	19%		404.00	492.00	177.09	22%
	312.00	460.00	142.72	25%		492.00	598.00	214.88	25%
	460.00	576.00	195.60	30%		598.00	704.00	255.93	28%
	576.00	683.00	240.35	34%		704.00	917.00	323.82	33%
	683.00	....	276.24	37%		917.00	....	387.95	37%
2	$0	$124.00	$67.00	12%	**2**	$0	$232.00	$88.00	12%
	124.00	225.00	78.40	15%		232.00	424.00	130.35	17%
	225.00	332.00	109.26	19%		424.00	512.00	197.09	22%
	332.00	480.00	162.72	25%		512.00	618.00	234.88	25%
	480.00	596.00	215.60	30%		618.00	724.00	275.93	28%
	596.00	703.00	260.35	34%		724.00	937.00	343.82	33%
	703.00	....	296.24	37%		937.00	....	407.95	37%
3	$0	$144.00	$87.00	12%	**3**	$0	$252.00	$108.00	12%
	144.00	245.00	98.40	15%		252.00	444.00	150.35	17%
	245.00	352.00	129.26	19%		444.00	532.00	217.09	22%
	352.00	500.00	182.72	25%		532.00	638.00	254.88	25%
	500.00	616.00	235.60	30%		638.00	744.00	295.93	28%
	616.00	723.00	280.35	34%		744.00	957.00	363.82	33%
	723.00	....	316.24	37%		957.00	....	427.95	37%
4	$0	$164.00	$107.00	12%	**4**	$0	$272.00	$128.00	12%
	164.00	265.00	118.40	15%		272.00	464.00	170.35	17%
	265.00	372.00	149.26	19%		464.00	552.00	237.09	22%
	372.00	520.00	202.72	25%		552.00	658.00	274.88	25%
	520.00	636.00	255.60	30%		658.00	764.00	315.93	28%
	636.00	743.00	300.35	34%		764.00	977.00	383.82	33%
	743.00	....	336.24	37%		977.00	....	447.95	37%
5	$0	$184.00	$127.00	12%	**5**	$0	$292.00	$148.00	12%
	184.00	285.00	138.40	15%		292.00	484.00	190.35	17%
	285.00	392.00	169.26	19%		484.00	572.00	257.09	22%
	392.00	540.00	222.72	25%		572.00	678.00	294.88	25%
	540.00	656.00	275.60	30%		678.00	784.00	335.93	28%
	656.00	763.00	320.35	34%		784.00	997.00	403.82	33%
	763.00	....	356.24	37%		997.00	....	467.95	37%
6	$0	$204.00	$147.00	12%	**6**	$0	$312.00	$168.00	12%
	204.00	305.00	158.40	15%		312.00	504.00	210.35	17%
	305.00	412.00	189.26	19%		504.00	592.00	277.09	22%
	412.00	560.00	242.72	25%		592.00	698.00	314.88	25%
	560.00	676.00	295.60	30%		698.00	804.00	355.93	28%
	676.00	783.00	340.35	34%		804.00	1,017.00	423.82	33%
	783.00	....	376.24	37%		1,017.00	....	487.95	37%
7	$0	$224.00	$167.00	12%	**7**	$0	$332.00	$188.00	12%
	224.00	325.00	178.40	15%		332.00	524.00	230.35	17%
	325.00	432.00	209.26	19%		524.00	612.00	297.09	22%
	432.00	580.00	262.72	25%		612.00	718.00	334.88	25%
	580.00	696.00	315.60	30%		718.00	824.00	375.93	28%
	696.00	803.00	360.35	34%		824.00	1,037.00	443.82	33%
	803.00	....	396.24	37%		1,037.00	....	507.95	37%
8	$0	$244.00	$187.00	12%	**8**	$0	$352.00	$208.00	12%
	244.00	345.00	198.40	15%		352.00	544.00	250.35	17%
	345.00	452.00	229.26	19%		544.00	632.00	317.09	22%
	452.00	600.00	282.72	25%		632.00	738.00	354.88	25%
	600.00	716.00	335.60	30%		738.00	844.00	395.93	28%
	716.00	823.00	380.35	34%		844.00	1,057.00	463.82	33%
	823.00	....	416.24	37%		1,057.00	....	527.95	37%
9[2]	$0	$264.00	$207.00	12%	**9**[2]	$0	$372.00	$228.00	12%
	264.00	365.00	218.40	15%		372.00	564.00	270.35	17%
	365.00	472.00	249.26	19%		564.00	652.00	337.09	22%
	472.00	620.00	302.72	25%		652.00	758.00	374.88	25%
	620.00	736.00	355.60	30%		758.00	864.00	415.93	28%
	736.00	843.00	400.35	34%		864.00	1,077.00	483.82	33%
	843.00	....	436.24	37%		1,077.00	....	547.95	37%

Instructions

A. For each employee, use the appropriate payroll period table and marital status section and select the subsection showing the number of allowances claimed.

B. Read across the selected subsection and locate the wage bracket range applicable to the employee's gross wage.

C. From the employee's gross wage, subtract the amount shown on the next column of the appropriate row.

D. Multiply the remaining amount of wages by the withholding percentage rate shown in the last column. The result of this computation is the amount of tax to be withheld.

[1] If the gross wages are less than the amount to be subtracted, the withholding is zero.

[2] You can expand these tables for additional allowances. To do this, increase the wage bracket and subtraction amounts in this subsection by $20.00 for each additional allowance claimed.

(For Wages Paid After December 1984)

Wage Bracket Percentage Method Table for Computing
Income Tax Withholding from Gross Wages

Biweekly Payroll Period

Single Persons

If the number of allowances is—	And gross wages are— Over	But not over	Subtract from gross wages [1]	Multiply remainder by—
0	$0	$168.00	$55.00	12%
	168.00	369.00	77.60	15%
	369.00	585.00	138.95	19%
	585.00	881.00	246.00	25%
	881.00	1,113.00	351.83	30%
	1,113.00	1,325.00	441.38	34%
	1,325.00	....	513.03	37%
1	$0	$208.00	$95.00	12%
	208.00	409.00	117.60	15%
	409.00	625.00	178.95	19%
	625.00	921.00	286.00	25%
	921.00	1,153.00	391.83	30%
	1,153.00	1,365.00	481.38	34%
	1,365.00	....	553.03	37%
2	$0	$248.00	$135.00	12%
	248.00	449.00	157.60	15%
	449.00	665.00	218.95	19%
	665.00	961.00	326.00	25%
	961.00	1,193.00	431.83	30%
	1,193.00	1,405.00	521.38	34%
	1,405.00	....	593.03	37%
3	$0	$288.00	$175.00	12%
	288.00	489.00	197.60	15%
	489.00	705.00	258.95	19%
	705.00	1,001.00	366.00	25%
	1,001.00	1,233.00	471.83	30%
	1,233.00	1,445.00	561.38	34%
	1,445.00	....	633.03	37%
4	$0	$328.00	$215.00	12%
	328.00	529.00	237.60	15%
	529.00	745.00	298.95	19%
	745.00	1,041.00	406.00	25%
	1,041.00	1,273.00	511.83	30%
	1,273.00	1,485.00	601.38	34%
	1,485.00	....	673.03	37%
5	$0	$368.00	$255.00	12%
	368.00	569.00	277.60	15%
	569.00	785.00	338.95	19%
	785.00	1,081.00	446.00	25%
	1,081.00	1,313.00	551.83	30%
	1,313.00	1,525.00	641.38	34%
	1,525.00	....	713.03	37%
6	$0	$408.00	$295.00	12%
	408.00	609.00	317.60	15%
	609.00	825.00	378.95	19%
	825.00	1,121.00	486.00	25%
	1,121.00	1,353.00	591.83	30%
	1,353.00	1,565.00	681.38	34%
	1,565.00	....	753.03	37%
7	$0	$448.00	$335.00	12%
	448.00	649.00	357.60	15%
	649.00	865.00	418.95	19%
	865.00	1,161.00	526.00	25%
	1,161.00	1,393.00	631.83	30%
	1,393.00	1,605.00	721.38	34%
	1,605.00	....	793.03	37%
8	$0	$488.00	$375.00	12%
	488.00	689.00	397.60	15%
	689.00	905.00	458.95	19%
	905.00	1,201.00	566.00	25%
	1,201.00	1,433.00	671.83	30%
	1,433.00	1,645.00	761.38	34%
	1,645.00	....	833.03	37%
9 [2]	$0	$528.00	$415.00	12%
	528.00	729.00	437.60	15%
	729.00	945.00	498.95	19%
	945.00	1,241.00	606.00	25%
	1,241.00	1,473.00	711.83	30%
	1,473.00	1,685.00	801.38	34%
	1,685.00	....	873.03	37%

Married Persons

If the number of allowances is—	And gross wages are— Over	But not over	Subtract from gross wages [1]	Multiply remainder by—
0	$0	$385.00	$96.00	12%
	385.00	767.00	181.00	17%
	767.00	945.00	314.18	22%
	945.00	1,157.00	389.88	25%
	1,157.00	1,369.00	472.07	28%
	1,369.00	1,793.00	607.97	33%
	1,793.00	....	736.08	37%
1	$0	$425.00	$136.00	12%
	425.00	807.00	221.00	17%
	807.00	985.00	354.18	22%
	985.00	1,197.00	429.88	25%
	1,197.00	1,409.00	512.07	28%
	1,409.00	1,833.00	647.97	33%
	1,833.00	....	776.08	37%
2	$0	$465.00	$176.00	12%
	465.00	847.00	261.00	17%
	847.00	1,025.00	394.18	22%
	1,025.00	1,237.00	469.88	25%
	1,237.00	1,449.00	552.07	28%
	1,449.00	1,873.00	687.97	33%
	1,873.00	....	816.08	37%
3	$0	$505.00	$216.00	12%
	505.00	887.00	301.00	17%
	887.00	1,065.00	434.18	22%
	1,065.00	1,277.00	509.88	25%
	1,277.00	1,489.00	592.07	28%
	1,489.00	1,913.00	727.97	33%
	1,913.00	....	856.08	37%
4	$0	$545.00	$256.00	12%
	545.00	927.00	341.00	17%
	927.00	1,105.00	474.18	22%
	1,105.00	1,317.00	549.88	25%
	1,317.00	1,529.00	632.07	28%
	1,529.00	1,953.00	767.97	33%
	1,953.00	....	896.08	37%
5	$0	$585.00	$296.00	12%
	585.00	967.00	381.00	17%
	967.00	1,145.00	514.18	22%
	1,145.00	1,357.00	589.88	25%
	1,357.00	1,569.00	672.07	28%
	1,569.00	1,993.00	807.97	33%
	1,993.00	....	936.08	37%
6	$0	$625.00	$336.00	12%
	625.00	1,007.00	421.00	17%
	1,007.00	1,185.00	554.18	22%
	1,185.00	1,397.00	629.88	25%
	1,397.00	1,609.00	712.07	28%
	1,609.00	2,033.00	847.97	33%
	2,033.00	....	976.08	37%
7	$0	$665.00	$376.00	12%
	665.00	1,047.00	461.00	17%
	1,047.00	1,225.00	594.18	22%
	1,225.00	1,437.00	669.88	25%
	1,437.00	1,649.00	752.07	28%
	1,649.00	2,073.00	887.97	33%
	2,073.00	....	1,016.08	37%
8	$0	$705.00	$416.00	12%
	705.00	1,087.00	501.00	17%
	1,087.00	1,265.00	634.18	22%
	1,265.00	1,477.00	709.88	25%
	1,477.00	1,689.00	792.07	28%
	1,689.00	2,113.00	927.97	33%
	2,113.00	....	1,056.08	37%
9 [2]	$0	$745.00	$456.00	12%
	745.00	1,127.00	541.00	17%
	1,127.00	1,305.00	674.18	22%
	1,305.00	1,517.00	749.88	25%
	1,517.00	1,729.00	832.07	28%
	1,729.00	2,153.00	967.97	33%
	2,153.00	....	1,096.08	37%

Instructions

A. For each employee, use the appropriate payroll period table and marital status section and select the subsection showing the number of allowances claimed.

B. Read across the selected subsection and locate the wage bracket range applicable to the employee's gross wage.

C. From the employee's gross wage, subtract the amount shown on the next column of the appropriate row.

D. Multiply the remaining amount of wages by the withholding percentage rate shown in the last column. The result of this computation is the amount of tax to be withheld.

[1] If the gross wages are less than the amount to be subtracted, the withholding is zero.

[2] You can expand these tables for additional allowances. To do this, increase the wage bracket and subtraction amounts in this subsection by $40.00 for each additional allowance claimed.

(For Wages Paid After December 1984)

Wage Bracket Percentage Method Table for Computing
Income Tax Withholding from Gross Wages

Semimonthly Payroll Period

Single Persons

If the number of allowances is—	And gross wages are— Over	But not over	Subtract from gross wages [1]	Multiply remainder by—
0	$0	$182.00	$59.00	12%
	182.00	400.00	83.60	15%
	400.00	633.00	150.21	19%
	633.00	954.00	266.08	25%
	954.00	1,205.00	380.73	30%
	1,205.00	1,435.00	477.71	34%
	1,435.00	....	555.32	37%
1	$0	$225.33	$102.33	12%
	225.33	443.33	126.93	15%
	443.33	676.33	193.54	19%
	676.33	997.33	309.41	25%
	997.33	1,248.33	424.06	30%
	1,248.33	1,478.33	521.04	34%
	1,478.33	....	598.65	37%
2	$0	$268.66	$145.66	12%
	268.66	486.66	170.26	15%
	486.66	719.66	236.87	19%
	719.66	1,040.66	352.74	25%
	1,040.66	1,291.66	467.39	30%
	1,291.66	1,521.66	564.37	34%
	1,521.66	....	641.98	37%
3	$0	$311.99	$188.99	12%
	311.99	529.99	213.59	15%
	529.99	762.99	280.20	19%
	762.99	1,083.99	396.07	25%
	1,083.99	1,334.99	510.72	30%
	1,334.99	1,564.99	607.70	34%
	1,564.99	....	685.31	37%
4	$0	$355.32	$232.32	12%
	355.32	573.32	256.92	15%
	573.32	806.32	323.53	19%
	806.32	1,127.32	439.40	25%
	1,127.32	1,378.32	554.05	30%
	1,378.32	1,608.32	651.03	34%
	1,608.32	....	728.64	37%
5	$0	$398.65	$275.65	12%
	398.65	616.65	300.25	15%
	616.65	849.65	366.86	19%
	849.65	1,170.65	482.73	25%
	1,170.65	1,421.65	597.38	30%
	1,421.65	1,651.65	694.36	34%
	1,651.65	....	771.97	37%
6	$0	$441.98	$318.98	12%
	441.98	659.98	343.58	15%
	659.98	892.98	410.19	19%
	892.98	1,213.98	526.06	25%
	1,213.98	1,464.98	640.71	30%
	1,464.98	1,694.98	737.69	34%
	1,694.98	....	815.30	37%
7	$0	$485.31	$362.31	12%
	485.31	703.31	386.91	15%
	703.31	936.31	453.52	19%
	936.31	1,257.31	569.39	25%
	1,257.31	1,508.31	684.04	30%
	1,508.31	1,738.31	781.02	34%
	1,738.31	....	858.63	37%
8	$0	$528.64	$405.64	12%
	528.64	746.64	430.24	15%
	746.64	979.64	496.85	19%
	979.64	1,300.64	612.72	25%
	1,300.64	1,551.64	727.37	30%
	1,551.64	1,781.64	824.35	34%
	1,781.64	....	901.96	37%
9 [2]	$0	$571.97	$448.97	12%
	571.97	789.97	473.57	15%
	789.97	1,022.97	540.18	19%
	1,022.97	1,343.97	656.05	25%
	1,343.97	1,594.97	770.70	30%
	1,594.97	1,824.97	867.68	34%
	1,824.97	....	945.29	37%

Married Persons

If the number of allowances is—	And gross wages are— Over	But not over	Subtract from gross wages [1]	Multiply remainder by—
0	$0	$417.00	$104.00	12%
	417.00	831.00	196.06	17%
	831.00	1,023.00	340.36	22%
	1,023.00	1,253.00	422.28	25%
	1,253.00	1,483.00	511.29	28%
	1,483.00	1,943.00	658.52	33%
	1,943.00	....	797.38	37%
1	$0	$460.33	$147.33	12%
	460.33	874.33	239.39	17%
	874.33	1,066.33	383.69	22%
	1,066.33	1,296.33	465.61	25%
	1,296.33	1,526.33	554.62	28%
	1,526.33	1,986.33	701.85	33%
	1,986.33	....	840.71	37%
2	$0	$503.66	$190.66	12%
	503.66	917.66	282.72	17%
	917.66	1,109.66	427.02	22%
	1,109.66	1,339.66	508.94	25%
	1,339.66	1,569.66	597.95	28%
	1,569.66	2,029.66	745.18	33%
	2,029.66	....	884.04	37%
3	$0	$546.99	$233.99	12%
	546.99	960.99	326.05	17%
	960.99	1,152.99	470.35	22%
	1,152.99	1,382.99	552.27	25%
	1,382.99	1,612.99	641.28	28%
	1,612.99	2,072.99	788.51	33%
	2,072.99	....	927.37	37%
4	$0	$590.32	$277.32	12%
	590.32	1,004.32	369.38	17%
	1,004.32	1,196.32	513.68	22%
	1,196.32	1,426.32	595.60	25%
	1,426.32	1,656.32	684.61	28%
	1,656.32	2,116.32	831.84	33%
	2,116.32	....	970.70	37%
5	$0	$633.65	$320.65	12%
	633.65	1,047.65	412.71	17%
	1,047.65	1,239.65	557.01	22%
	1,239.65	1,469.65	638.93	25%
	1,469.65	1,699.65	727.94	28%
	1,699.65	2,159.65	875.17	33%
	2,159.65	....	1,014.03	37%
6	$0	$676.98	$363.98	12%
	676.98	1,090.98	456.04	17%
	1,090.98	1,282.98	600.34	22%
	1,282.98	1,512.98	682.26	25%
	1,512.98	1,742.98	771.27	28%
	1,742.98	2,202.98	918.50	33%
	2,202.98	....	1,057.36	37%
7	$0	$720.31	$407.31	12%
	720.31	1,134.31	499.37	17%
	1,134.31	1,326.31	643.67	22%
	1,326.31	1,556.31	725.59	25%
	1,556.31	1,786.31	814.60	28%
	1,786.31	2,246.31	961.83	33%
	2,246.31	....	1,100.69	37%
8	$0	$763.64	$450.64	12%
	763.64	1,177.64	542.70	17%
	1,177.64	1,369.64	687.00	22%
	1,369.64	1,599.64	768.92	25%
	1,599.64	1,829.64	857.93	28%
	1,829.64	2,289.64	1,005.16	33%
	2,289.64	....	1,144.02	37%
9 [2]	$0	$806.97	$493.97	12%
	806.97	1,220.97	586.03	17%
	1,220.97	1,412.97	730.33	22%
	1,412.97	1,642.97	812.25	25%
	1,642.97	1,872.97	901.26	28%
	1,872.97	2,332.97	1,048.49	33%
	2,332.97	....	1,187.35	37%

Instructions

A. For each employee, use the appropriate payroll period table and marital status section and select the subsection showing the number of allowances claimed.

B. Read across the selected subsection and locate the wage bracket range applicable to the employee's gross wage.

C. From the employee's gross wage, subtract the amount shown on the next column of the appropriate row.

D. Multiply the remaining amount of wages by the withholding percentage rate shown in the last column. The result of this computation is the amount of tax to be withheld.

[1] If the gross wages are less than the amount to be subtracted, withholding is zero.

[2] You can expand these tables for additional allowances. To do this, increase the wage bracket and subtraction amounts in this subsection by $43.33 for each additional allowance claimed.

(For Wages Paid After December 1984)

Wage Bracket Percentage Method Table for Computing
Income Tax Withholding from Gross Wages

Monthly Payroll Period

	Single Persons					Married Persons			
If the number of allowances is–	And gross wages are– Over	But not over	Subtract from gross wages [1]	Multiply remainder by–	If the number of allowances is–	And gross wages are– Over	But not over	Subtract from gross wages [1]	Multiply remainder by–
0	$0	$364.00	$118.00	12%	**0**	$0	$833.00	$208.00	12%
	364.00	800.00	167.20	15%		833.00	1,663.00	391.82	17%
	800.00	1,267.00	300.42	19%		1,663.00	2,047.00	680.73	22%
	1,267.00	1,908.00	532.40	25%		2,047.00	2,507.00	844.68	25%
	1,908.00	2,411.00	761.67	30%		2,507.00	2,966.00	1,022.79	28%
	2,411.00	2,871.00	955.71	34%		2,966.00	3,885.00	1,317.21	33%
	2,871.00	....	1,111.00	37%		3,885.00	....	1,594.81	37%
1	$0	$450.67	$204.67	12%	**1**	$0	$919.67	$294.67	12%
	450.67	886.67	253.87	15%		919.67	1,749.67	478.49	17%
	886.67	1,353.67	387.09	19%		1,749.67	2,133.67	767.40	22%
	1,353.67	1,994.67	619.07	25%		2,133.67	2,593.67	931.35	25%
	1,994.67	2,497.67	848.34	30%		2,593.67	3,052.67	1,109.46	28%
	2,497.67	2,957.67	1,042.38	34%		3,052.67	3,971.67	1,403.88	33%
	2,957.67	....	1,197.67	37%		3,971.67	....	1,681.48	37%
2	$0	$537.34	$291.34	12%	**2**	$0	$1,006.34	$381.34	12%
	537.34	973.34	340.54	15%		1,006.34	1,836.34	565.16	17%
	973.34	1,440.34	473.76	19%		1,836.34	2,220.34	854.07	22%
	1,440.34	2,081.34	705.74	25%		2,220.34	2,680.34	1,018.02	25%
	2,081.34	2,584.34	935.01	30%		2,680.34	3,139.34	1,196.13	28%
	2,584.34	3,044.34	1,129.05	34%		3,139.34	4,058.34	1,490.55	33%
	3,044.34	....	1,284.34	37%		4,058.34	....	1,768.15	37%
3	$0	$624.01	$378.01	12%	**3**	$0	$1,093.01	$468.01	12%
	624.01	1,060.01	427.21	15%		1,093.01	1,923.01	651.83	17%
	1,060.01	1,527.01	560.43	19%		1,923.01	2,307.01	940.74	22%
	1,527.01	2,168.01	792.41	25%		2,307.01	2,767.01	1,104.69	25%
	2,168.01	2,671.01	1,021.68	30%		2,767.01	3,226.01	1,282.80	28%
	2,671.01	3,131.01	1,215.72	34%		3,226.01	4,145.01	1,577.22	33%
	3,131.01	....	1,371.01	37%		4,145.01	....	1,854.82	37%
4	$0	$710.68	$464.68	12%	**4**	$0	$1,179.68	$554.68	12%
	710.68	1,146.68	513.88	15%		1,179.68	2,009.68	738.50	17%
	1,146.68	1,613.68	647.10	19%		2,009.68	2,393.68	1,027.41	22%
	1,613.68	2,254.68	879.08	25%		2,393.68	2,853.68	1,191.36	25%
	2,254.68	2,757.68	1,108.35	30%		2,853.68	3,312.68	1,369.47	28%
	2,757.68	3,217.68	1,302.39	34%		3,312.68	4,231.68	1,663.89	33%
	3,217.68	....	1,457.68	37%		4,231.68	....	1,941.49	37%
5	$0	$797.35	$551.35	12%	**5**	$0	$1,266.35	$641.35	12%
	797.35	1,233.35	600.55	15%		1,266.35	2,096.35	825.17	17%
	1,233.35	1,700.35	733.77	19%		2,096.35	2,480.35	1,114.08	22%
	1,700.35	2,341.35	965.75	25%		2,480.35	2,940.35	1,278.03	25%
	2,341.35	2,844.35	1,195.02	30%		2,940.35	3,399.35	1,456.14	28%
	2,844.35	3,304.35	1,389.06	34%		3,399.35	4,318.35	1,750.56	33%
	3,304.35	....	1,544.35	37%		4,318.35	....	2,028.16	37%
6	$0	$884.02	$638.02	12%	**6**	$0	$1,353.02	$728.02	12%
	884.02	1,320.02	687.22	15%		1,353.02	2,183.02	911.84	17%
	1,320.02	1,787.02	820.44	19%		2,183.02	2,567.02	1,200.75	22%
	1,787.02	2,428.02	1,052.42	25%		2,567.02	3,027.02	1,364.70	25%
	2,428.02	2,931.02	1,281.69	30%		3,027.02	3,486.02	1,542.81	28%
	2,931.02	3,391.02	1,475.73	34%		3,486.02	4,405.02	1,837.23	33%
	3,391.02	....	1,631.02	37%		4,405.02	....	2,114.83	37%
7	$0	$970.69	$724.69	12%	**7**	$0	$1,439.69	$814.69	12%
	970.69	1,406.69	773.89	15%		1,439.69	2,269.69	998.51	17%
	1,406.69	1,873.69	907.11	19%		2,269.69	2,653.69	1,287.42	22%
	1,873.69	2,514.69	1,139.09	25%		2,653.69	3,113.69	1,451.37	25%
	2,514.69	3,017.69	1,368.36	30%		3,113.69	3,572.69	1,629.48	28%
	3,017.69	3,477.69	1,562.40	34%		3,572.69	4,491.69	1,923.90	33%
	3,477.69	....	1,717.69	37%		4,491.69	....	2,201.50	37%
8	$0	$1,057.36	$811.36	12%	**8**	$0	$1,526.36	$901.36	12%
	1,057.36	1,493.36	860.56	15%		1,526.36	2,356.36	1,085.18	17%
	1,493.36	1,960.36	993.78	19%		2,356.36	2,740.36	1,374.09	22%
	1,960.36	2,601.36	1,225.76	25%		2,740.36	3,200.36	1,538.04	25%
	2,601.36	3,104.36	1,455.03	30%		3,200.36	3,659.36	1,716.15	28%
	3,104.36	3,564.36	1,649.07	34%		3,659.36	4,578.36	2,010.57	33%
	3,564.36	....	1,804.36	37%		4,578.36	....	2,288.17	37%
9 [2]	$0	$1,144.03	$898.03	12%	**9** [2]	$0	$1,613.03	$988.03	12%
	1,144.03	1,580.03	947.23	15%		1,613.03	2,443.03	1,171.85	17%
	1,580.03	2,047.03	1,080.45	19%		2,443.03	2,827.03	1,460.76	22%
	2,047.03	2,688.03	1,312.43	25%		2,827.03	3,287.03	1,624.71	25%
	2,688.03	3,191.03	1,541.70	30%		3,287.03	3,746.03	1,802.82	28%
	3,191.03	3,651.03	1,735.74	34%		3,746.03	4,665.03	2,097.24	33%
	3,651.03	....	1,891.03	37%		4,665.03	....	2,374.84	37%

Instructions

A. For each employee, use the appropriate payroll period table and marital status section and select the subsection showing the number of allowances claimed.

B. Read across the selected subsection and locate the wage bracket range applicable to the employee's gross wage.

C. From the employee's gross wage, subtract the amount shown on the next column of the appropriate row.

D. Multiply the remaining amount of wages by the withholding percentage rate shown in the last column. The result of this computation is the amount of tax to be withheld.

[1] If the gross wages are less than the amount to be subtracted, the withholding is zero.

[2] You can expand these tables for additional allowances. To do this, increase the wage bracket and subtraction amounts in this subsection by $86.67 for each additional allowance claimed.

Appendix 2: 1985 Tax Rate Schedules

1985 Tax Rate Schedules

Caution: Do not use these Tax Rate Schedules to figure your 1984 taxes. Use only to figure your 1985 estimated taxes.

SCHEDULE X—Single Taxpayers

If line 5 is: Over—	but not over—	The tax is:	of the amount over—
$0	$2,390	—0—	
2,390	3,540	······· 11%	$2,390
3,540	4,580	$126.50 + 12%	3,540
4,580	6,760	251.30 + 14%	4,580
6,760	8,850	556.50 + 15%	6,760
8,850	11,240	870.00 + 16%	8,850
11,240	13,430	1,252.40 + 18%	11,240
13,430	15,610	1,646.60 + 20%	13,430
15,610	18,940	2,082.60 + 23%	15,610
18,940	24,460	2,848.50 + 26%	18,940
24,460	29,970	4,283.70 + 30%	24,460
29,970	35,490	5,936.70 + 34%	29,970
35,490	43,190	7,813.50 + 38%	35,490
43,190	57,550	10,739.50 + 42%	43,190
57,550	85,130	16,770.70 + 48%	57,550
85,130	········	30,009.10 + 50%	85,130

SCHEDULE Z—Heads of Household

If line 5 is: Over—	but not over—	The tax is:	of the amount over—
$0	$2,390	—0—	
2,390	4,580	······· 11%	$2,390
4,580	6,760	$240.90 + 12%	4,580
6,760	9,050	502.50 + 14%	6,760
9,050	12,280	823.10 + 17%	9,050
12,280	15,610	1,372.20 + 18%	12,280
15,610	18,940	1,971.60 + 20%	15,610
18,940	24,460	2,637.60 + 24%	18,940
24,460	29,970	3,962.40 + 28%	24,460
29,970	35,490	5,505.20 + 32%	29,970
35,490	46,520	7,271.60 + 35%	35,490
46,520	63,070	11,132.10 + 42%	46,520
63,070	85,130	18,083.10 + 45%	63,070
85,130	112,720	28,010.10 + 48%	85,130
112,720	······	41,253.30 + 50%	112,720

SCHEDULE Y—Married Taxpayers and Qualifying Widows and Widowers

Married Filing Joint Returns and Qualifying Widows and Widowers

If line 5 is: Over—	but not over—	The tax is:	of the amount over—
$0	$3,540	—0—	
3,540	5,720	······· 11%	$3,540
5,720	7,910	$239.80 + 12%	5,720
7,910	12,390	502.60 + 14%	7,910
12,390	16,650	1,129.80 + 16%	12,390
16,650	21,020	1,811.40 + 18%	16,650
21,020	25,600	2,598.00 + 22%	21,020
25,600	31,120	3,605.60 + 25%	25,600
31,120	36,630	4,985.60 + 28%	31,120
36,630	47,670	6,528.40 + 33%	36,630
47,670	62,450	10,171.60 + 38%	47,670
62,450	89,090	15,788.00 + 42%	62,450
89,090	113,860	26,976.80 + 45%	89,090
113,860	169,020	38,123.30 + 49%	113,860
169,020	········	65,151.70 + 50%	169,020

Married Filing Separate Returns

If line 5 is: Over—	but not over—	The tax is:	of the amount over—
$0	$1,770	—0—	
1,770	2,860	······· 11%	1,770
2,860	3,955	$119.90 + 12%	2,860
3,955	6,195	251.30 + 14%	3,955
6,195	8,325	564.90 + 16%	6,195
8,325	10,510	905.70 + 18%	8,325
10,510	12,800	1,299.00 + 22%	10,510
12,800	15,560	1,802.80 + 25%	12,800
15,560	18,315	2,492.80 + 28%	15,560
18,315	23,835	3,264.20 + 33%	18,315
23,835	31,225	5,085.80 + 38%	23,835
31,225	44,545	7,894.00 + 42%	31,225
44,545	56,930	13,488.40 + 45%	44,545
56,930	84,510	19,061.65 + 49%	56,930
84,510	······	32,575.85 + 50%	84,510